THE REAL READER'S QUARTERLY

Slightly Foxed

'Underwater Heaven'

NO.66   SUMMER 2020

Editors Gail Pirkis & Hazel Wood
Marketing and publicity Stephanie Allen & Jennie Harrison Bunning
Bookshops Anna Kirk
Subscriptions Hattie Summers & Jess Dalby

Cover illustration Paul Cleden, 'Boats and Coots', linocut

Paul Cleden is an illustrator and printmaker who is especially drawn to figurative movement – the dynamic shapes of cyclists or skiers, rowers or divers, but equally a crowd at rush hour leaving a train or a dance hall crowded with figures. In depicting such scenes his use of linocut allows for beautiful flowing lines and the dramatic overlap of colours. His work can be seen in galleries across the UK and in commissions from, among others, the National Trust and the Royal Society for the Protection of Birds. For more see his website www.paulcleden.co.uk.

Back cover fox by Paul Cleden
Design by Octavius Murray
Layout by Andrew Evans
Colophon and tailpiece by David Eccles

Published by Slightly Foxed Limited
53 Hoxton Square
London N1 6PB

tel 020 7033 0258
email office@foxedquarterly.com
www.foxedquarterly.com

Slightly Foxed is published quarterly in early March, June, September and December

Annual subscription rates (4 issues)
UK and Ireland £48; Overseas £56

Single copies of this issue can be bought for £12.50 (UK) or £14.50 (Overseas)

All back issues in printed form are also available

ISBN 978-1-910898-42-0
ISSN 1742-5794

Printed and bound by Smith Settle, Yeadon, West Yorkshire

Contents

From the Editors   5

Underwater Heaven · MARGARET DRABBLE
   Charles Kingsley, *The Water-Babies*   7

'What larks!' · ANTONY WOOD
   Christopher Robbins, *The Empress of Ireland*   13

Hazy Memories of Hanging Rock · KATE YOUNG
   Joan Lindsay, *Picnic at Hanging Rock*   19

Simply Delicious · CLIVE UNGER-HAMILTON
   Theodora FitzGibbon, *A Taste of Paris*   25

An Outsider in Tregonissey · ANNABEL WALKER
   A. L. Rowse, *A Cornish Childhood*   29

Partying down at the Palace · MICK HERRON
   John Steinbeck, *Sweet Thursday* & *Cannery Row*   35

These Fragments · JON WOOLCOTT
   John Harris, *No Voice from the Hall*   40

On the Shoulders of Giants · ANDREW JOYNES
   T. H. White, *England Have My Bones*   46

A Long Way from Surrey · SIMON WINDER
   H. G. Wells, *The Island of Doctor Moreau*   52

A Hot-Water Bottle and a Horse · SARAH CROWDEN
   Penelope Chetwode, *Two Middle-Aged Ladies in Andalusia*   57

Contents

Labours of Love · PAUL EDWARDS
Alan Ross, *Coastwise Lights*   61

An Early-Flowering Climber · URSULA BUCHAN
The plant-hunting and garden writings of Reginald Farrer   68

Nothing but the Best · DANIEL WORSLEY
Iris Origo, *The Merchant of Prato*   73

Keeping up Appearances · KATE TYTE
Eve Garnett, *The Family from One End Street*   79

A Modern Prospero · BRANDON ROBSHAW
Iris Murdoch, *The Sea, The Sea*   84

Life among the Ledgers · PAULINE MELVILLE
Herman Melville, 'Bartleby, the Scrivener: A Story of Wall Street'   89

Bibliography   94

John Watson

The Slightly Foxed Podcast

A new episode of our podcast is available on the 15th of every month. To listen, visit www.foxedquarterly.com/pod or search for Slightly Foxed on Audioboom, iTunes or your podcast app.

Subscriber Benefits

Slightly Foxed can obtain any books reviewed in this issue, whether new or second-hand. To enquire about a book, to access the digital edition of *Slightly Foxed* or to view a list of membership benefits, visit www.foxedquarterly.com/members or contact the office: 020 7033 0258/office@foxedquarterly.com.

From the Editors

As we write this, towards the end of April, we are still in total lock-down because of the coronavirus. In these difficult times, we'd like to say how very touched we've been by all the extra efforts you've been making to support us, writing to us, extending your subscriptions and buying more books. It's something we'll never forget.

We must confess that most evenings these days we both escape to Ambridge, the setting for our shared addiction *The Archers*, BBC Radio 4's venerable 70-year-old soap set in a rural community some-where in the heart of England, which so far remains blissfully unaffected by grim events in the outside world. As those of you who have opted to receive our regular email newsletter will know, we're keeping you in touch with what's happening here via an additional weekly diary. Many of you have told us, however, what a relief it is to escape to other times and places by opening *Slightly Foxed*, so we've decided that from now on we'll take our cue from *The Archers* and keep *SF* itself and our editorials, like Ambridge, coronavirus-free.

Ironically in the spring issue we mentioned that the number of Brits who bought a print book last year had increased as compared to 2018. Soon after came another bit of cheering news – that after decades of decline, the number of independent bookshops is on the up. Now of course these small businesses, like so many others, are taking a terrible hit. If your local bookshop is still managing to take phone and online orders, please, if you can, support them. They are such a precious resource in this increasingly impersonal digitized world.

On a much more cheerful note, our new Slightly Foxed Edition, *The Empress of Ireland* by Christopher Robbins (see p.13), is a perfect relaxing summer read. It's subtitled 'The chronicle of an unusual friendship' and it's difficult to imagine a more unlikely relationship than that between the 80-year-old gay Irish film director Brian Desmond Hurst and the very English and very innocent straight young journalist Robbins. One key thing they had in common was that they were both broke, though this was not immediately obvious to Robbins when, to his surprise, he was taken on as scriptwriter for the great religious epic that was, apparently, to crown Hurst's career – a commission for which he was spectacularly ill-suited. His account of what followed as together they lived out this fantasy is both a comic masterpiece and a glorious portrait of an unapologetic but irresistible old rogue.

This month we're also reissuing one of our favourite SFEs in a Plain Foxed Edition, Christabel Bielenberg's riveting *The Past Is Myself*, a story of a very different kind. Christabel, from an influential Anglo-Irish family, met the liberal young lawyer Peter Bielenberg in Hamburg where she was studying singing and they married in 1934. They moved to Berlin and in 1942, when Allied bombing made the city too dangerous, Christabel fled to a remote village in the German countryside with their three small sons. Her book gives an unexpected picture of their wartime life in a Germany where there were few shortages, friendly German neighbours and little sympathy for the Nazi Party. She also describes her own daring confrontation with the Gestapo after Peter was arrested for his connection with Adam von Trott, one of the conspirators in the failed plot to assassinate Hitler.

And finally a piece of happy *SF* news, the arrival of Blythe Harrison Bunning, born earlier this year to our dear Jennie and her husband Tom. Though we've both of us become grandparents in the decades since we started *SF*, she is the first baby born to a full-time member of our office staff – the first true *Slightly Foxed* cub.

GAIL PIRKIS & HAZEL WOOD

Underwater Heaven

MARGARET DRABBLE

All my life I have been deeply affected by the underwater world, by rock pools and streams and rivers. In 1949, when I was 10, my father gave me a book called *The Sea-Shore*, with 48 delicately coloured plates, which I would read again and again, gazing in wonder at the limpets and blennies and starfish and seaweeds and hermit crabs. We used to spend our summer holidays at Filey on the North Yorkshire coast, and enjoyed many hours of happiness exploring the pools on the Brigg, a rocky promontory that juts into the sea to the north of the curving sandy bay.

Each high tide submerged it, and its pools were replenished. The sense of renewal was mystical, purifying. 'The moving waters at their priestlike task of pure ablution round earth's human shores . . .' I didn't know those lines of Keats then, but I often say them to myself now. I still dream of the Brigg. Late in his life my father wrote a novel called *Scawsby* (1977) which is clearly set in Filey. He calls the Brigg 'the Reef', and his narrator says that it was the submerged ruins of a Roman jetty, but I'm not sure if that's true. Even so we were all enthralled by it.

I can't remember what age I was when I came across Charles Kingsley's *The Water-Babies*. I must have read it earlier than my other childhood favourite, Jules Verne's *20,000 Leagues under the Sea*, which was a

Charles Kingsley, *The Water-Babies* (1863) · Ed. Brian Alderson · Introd. Robert Douglas-Fairhurst
OUP · Pb · 288pp · £7.99 · ISBN 9780199685455

Christmas gift in 1948, but at that age I can't have tackled the Kingsley tale in its full version. I must have read a shortened illustrated children's text, of which there have been many. I loved the story of Tom's adventures, first as a dirty chimney-sweep intruding on little Ellie in her fine white bedchamber, then when he went on the run through a landscape that strangely mixes Yorkshire and Devon, then as a water-baby, as he ventures down the rivers and into the sea. I sympathized with his loneliness and with his longing to find other water-babies, and rejoiced with him when he discovered that the sea was full of them.

Most readers first come across the story in a children's version, as I did, and today there are several editions on sale, including one with sentimental illustrations by Mabel Lucie Atwell and another with W. Heath Robinson's quirky drawings. I didn't read the whole text until late middle age, when I was writing a novel about a marine biologist, a project that allowed me to indulge my longstanding interest in aquaria, deep-sea diving and aquatic ape theories. I was attracted by the evolutionary hypotheses of Elaine Morgan (1920–2013) who argued persistently and to me plausibly that human life originally evolved from the water, not from the savannah. Why else would we be naked and hairless, like seals and hippopotami? Why else do we sit lined up in deckchairs, gazing with longing at our primeval home? Of course we come from the water, and long to return to it.

In 2005 I was astonished by my first encounter with the original text of *The Water-Babies*, and I have just reread it in 2019 with more care and even more astonishment. It is one of the strangest stories ever written allegedly for children, even stranger than *Alice's Adventures in Wonderland*, which it predates by a couple of years. Ever since it first appeared, published by Macmillan in 1863, with two illustrations by the popular Scottish 'fantasy' artist Joseph Noel Paton, critics have debated as to whether it was intended for children (Kingsley claimed to have written it for his little boy Grenville Arthur) or whether it was really aimed, in a knowing way, at adults. It's interesting to note that Noel Paton's thumb-sucking water-babies are naked and mildly erotic, whereas in the story they are discreetly clothed in 'the neatest little white bathing-dresses'.

The book is packed with interesting information about river life and marine life, and with thrilling first-hand observations of fish and animal behaviour, all of which fit happily with the Victorian obsession with the seashore. Marine biology was a fashionable amateur pursuit in the 1850s and 1860s, and seaside resorts attracted adults and children to hunt for crabs and dabs. Philip Gosse, a pioneer in the field and author of the influential *A Naturalist's Ramble on the Devonshire Coast* (1853), was much admired by Kingsley, though they were to disagree fiercely about the Darwinian concept of evolution, which Gosse could not countenance but which Kingsley wholeheartedly embraced. To Kingsley, a devout clergyman and a passionate preacher and lecturer, there was no conflict between religion and evolution, and he believed that the myriad forms of life were a witness to the glory of God. He rejoiced in the oddities and eccentricities of creation.

The Water-Babies, in the person of the mysterious Mother Carey, presents perhaps the strangest and most eloquent personification of evolution in literature. Tom finds her in the arctic regions, towards the end of his long journey of purification. She is blue-eyed, white-haired, immensely aged, and she sits on a white marble throne, making her children out of sea water. Tom had expected to find her busy 'snipping, piecing, fitting, stitching, cobbling, basting, filing' but she sits still, with her chin upon her hand. Tom addresses her politely, apologizing for interrupting her, as he knows she is busy 'making new beasts out of old'. But she tells him that she is never busy. 'I am not going to trouble myself to make things, my little dear. I sit here and I make them make themselves.' It is a powerful image. I wonder what Richard Dawkins would make of her.

Some critical interpreters of *The Water-Babies* are repelled by what they see as its Victorian emphasis on guilt and punishment and its neurotic insistence that clean hands make pure minds. (Maureen Duffy, in *The Erotic World of Faery* (1972), provocatively sees Tom as a little questing penis.) Nobody could like Kingsley's jokes about the Irish, for he portrays them as an under-evolved race, and makes crude comments about apes and white gorillas and poor potato-eating Paddies. As the prototypical 'muscular Christian', he is very hard on any species he considers 'lazy'. Some critics take against his intrusive political agenda, his satirical onslaughts on current educational theory and practice, his Rabelaisian page-long lists and rollickingly inventive vocabulary – his coinages and usages are frequently cited in the *Oxford English Dictionary*. His references to contemporary debates about evolution and sanitation require a good many foot-notes, which are helpfully provided by the Oxford World's Classics 2013 edition, admirably edited by Brian Alderson, with an excellent introduction by Robert Douglas-Fairhurst. The jumble of scientific information and fantasy is undeniably odd, and Gillian Avery, the distinguished scholar of children's literature, found the book 'an inchoate mass'.

And so it is, but to me it is also a rich cabinet of curiosities. Kingsley's evocations of animals and fish life and insects, seen from tiny Tom's eft-like point of view, are masterly, and are based on many hours of first-hand observation from the riverbank or the shore. We meet the vain dragonfly, the proud and aged lobster whom Tom rescues from a lobster pot, the cruel otters, and the brave, dignified salmon who looks down on the lazy, cowardly, greedy trout, who choose 'to stay and poke about in the little streams and eat worms and grubs' instead of going down to the sea every year 'to see the world'. I even like the lists. One may be tempted to skip them on the page, but they could have been very entertaining when read aloud with brio to a fireside family audi-ence. And some of the scenes are very funny. There is a fine moment when the kindly but pedantic Professor Ptthmllnsprts is out beachcombing with little Ellie, who has been longing to see a water-baby, although assured by the professor that they do not exist. Even when he catches Tom in his net, he refuses to believe the evidence of his eyes, and classifies Tom, to Tom's great indignation, as 'a large pink Holothurian, with hands' or 'a Cephalopod'. Tom escapes the fate of being kept in an aquarium or pickled in a jar of spirits by biting the professor's finger until he lets him go.

The story navigates between the scientific observation of natural phenomena and a world of make-believe: as Kingsley says, 'this is all a fairy story, and only fun and pretence; and, therefore, you are not to believe a word of it, even if it is true'. At its best, it enters a mythic realm. Mrs Doasyouwouldbedoneby and Mrs Bedonebyasyoudid are well remembered and have become part of our folklore, but to me the finest passages are those that evoke the beauties of St Brandan's Isle, the home of the water-babies.

Imagining a desirable Christian heaven has proved notoriously difficult, but Kingsley sidesteps the issue by creating a semi-pagan underwater heaven-haven, an Isle of the Blessed beneath the sea. Kingsley's version of the legend tells us that St Brandan, having failed in his mission to convert the Irish, sailed away to the west to an earthly Paradise in the Atlantic, linked by Celtic mythology to Plato's lost Atlantis, where he preached to sea birds and fish and water-babies. Kingsley describes the flowers that come from the island – 'the Cornish heath, the Cornish moneywort, and the delicate Venus's hair, and the London-pride which covers the Kerry mountains, and the little pink butterwort of Devon . . .'

Even more wonderful than the flora are the rocks, for Tom found that

the isle stood on pillars, and that its roots were full of caves. There were pillars of black basalt, like Staffa; and pillars of green and crimson serpentine, like Kynance; and pillars ribboned with red and white and yellow sandstone, like Livermead . . . all curtained and draped with sea-weeds, purple and crimson, green and brown; and strewn with soft white sand, on which the water-babies sleep every night.

This is indeed very heaven. We can get quite close to it by visiting the Natural History Museum in Oxford, itself a cabinet of curiosities, where the cloisters and the carved stone piers and the pillars of alabaster and serpentine also bear witness to the Victorian love of the natural world, and sing to the glory of creation. The magnificent building belongs to exactly the same historical period as *The Water-Babies* and housed important debates on evolutionary biology. It is a Victorian wonderland, a brave new world of discovery.

MARGARET DRABBLE DBE is a novelist and critic. After a brief, inglorious career as an actress with the Royal Shakespeare Company she became a full-time writer. She is the author of nineteen novels, most recently *The Dark Flood Rises* (2016), and has also edited the Fifth and Sixth editions of the *Oxford Companion to English Literature.*
The illustrations in this piece are by W. Heath Robinson.

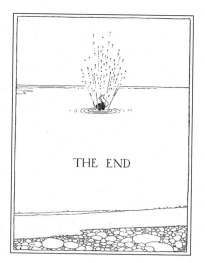

'What larks!'

ANTONY WOOD

'Your very good health, gentlemen! And by the way, gentlemen, I am *not* an old queen . . . *I am the Empress of Ireland!*'

It's mid-morning at the Turk's Head in Belgravia and Brian Desmond Hurst, a tall, distinguished-looking elderly figure, is replying to a trio of Guinness-drinkers who have greeted his entry to the bar by hissing the words 'Fucking old queen!' Nothing abashed, Hurst orders his usual breakfast glass of champagne with fresh orange juice and offers the Guinness drinkers a refill, which they shamefacedly accept. A suitable introduction to the hero (or is he the anti-hero?) of Christopher Robbins's uproarious *The Empress of Ireland* (2004) – a title I found irresistible when a friend showed me the book, which made me laugh as soon as I opened it and entertained me to the end.

Essentially it is the story of the friendship between Christopher Robbins, a struggling young freelance journalist, and Hurst, an ageing Irish film director who had already outlived his talents and gloriously continued to do so up to his death in 1986. For a delicious period of pure fantasy in the mid-1970s the two lived the life of Reilly together. When he first met Hurst the young Robbins was in his late twenties and vainly trying to claw his way out of perpetual debt. The agent of his introduction was an enigmatic American hipster masquerading as a German count whom he'd run into in Spain, and whose expertise was 'putting people together'.

The meeting took place as Hurst held court at a drunken lunch in his grandly shabby Georgian house in Kinnerton Street, Belgravia, through which passed an ever-changing stream of gay Guardsmen, artists, actors and social misfits, half of whom spoke in drawling upper-class tones and half in barrow-boy cockney. Although it was ten years since Hurst had made his last film (*The Playboy of the Western World,* 1962), it seemed the near-octogenarian was looking for a screenwriter for a new film. He was anxious to crown his career with a masterpiece, 'a Great Big Religious Picture . . . on the most important story of all. *The events leading up to* the birth of Christ'. Robbins was presented to him as a star, though knowing nothing of films or scriptwriting, and to his astonishment was immediately given the job.

But this is not a book about films or the making of films. Rather, it is an account of how a fixed idea can take over a person's life and mind, and it infectiously conveys the atmosphere of fantasy in which films are conceived and created. Its storyline is the duo's attempt to raise money for the new film, to find a suitable location for it, and lastly to achieve a script on what Hurst believes is a stunningly original subject: not the birth of Christ but '*the events leading up to it*'! We accompany the pair on three 'serious' trips abroad with these aims in mind – to Tangier, Malta and Ireland, the first being chosen for its plentiful supply of cheap extras ('all of them dressed in easily removed *djellabas*'), and the second for its homely familiarity as the setting for one of Hurst's best-known, or should one say today least unknown, films. The days are spent drinking champagne or fine wine (how this was paid for remains a mystery to the end). Hurst's memory is prodigious, and reminiscences and anecdotes pour forth from him in the course of conversations tête-à-tête or with potential backers and eccentric old acquaintances from his starrier days.

It is indeed a strange friendship between the somewhat naïve, straight young English journalist and the old outrageously camp Irish film director. But Robbins is dazzled both by Hurst's professional reputation and by the sheer heady irresponsibility of the life he leads.

Every journey undertaken, however insignificant, became a unique occasion promising glamour and adventure; even the deadly aspects of travel, such as hanging around airports and sitting on buses, were injected with a sense of fun. And no one enjoyed the experience more than Brian. As the taxi turned out of Kinnerton Street, at the start of each of our expeditions, he always said the same: 'Goody, goody – we're off!' He would then turn to me, blue eyes shining with boyish excitement: 'What larks, Christopher! What larks!'

Unsurprisingly, this routine does nothing to get a script started. After agonizing struggles, inspiration at last comes from T. S. Eliot's poem 'Journey of the Magi', the note being struck by the opening line, 'A cold coming we had of it . . .' Staggering in from a hot day on a Mediterranean beach, Robbins writes an opening screen-piece with 'visually powerful poetic images heavy with symbolism: sore-footed, bad-tempered camels collapsing in deep snow . . . sandalled feet kicking empty wineskins, as gnarled hands at a tavern door dice for pieces of silver'. Hurst thinks it  masterly – even when Robbins admits that the images come straight from Eliot's poem. The old film-maker doesn't turn a hair – 'Critics won't notice because it's not in the dialogue' – and gives an impromptu reading of the scene, which Robbins judges 'a bravura performance, subtle and nuanced, yet pure ham'.

Encouraged, the fledgling screenwriter next creates a diligently researched scene preceding Christ's birth ('The story was a corker . . .'). His conception centres on King Herod's unfortunate relations with his wife, the Hasmonean Queen Mariamne, with whose family he seriously falls out, eventually ordering Mariamne's murder. The Massacre of the Innocents occurs as one result of this family feud.

But the increasingly overloaded plot won't come together, and nor will any backer's money. The carefree spirit in which the quest for the latter is pursued is made plain at an important meeting between Hurst and a potential investor, a merchant banker whom Robbins has painstakingly cultivated after meeting him at a dinner party. The banker duly arrives at Kinnerton Street but before the meeting has a chance to take off, Brian is overcome by an irresistible urge to puncture the man's pomposity and casually suggests he take his clothes off, whereupon the outraged banker immediately leaves the house. It's one of the rare moments when Robbins loses his cool.

Hopes of progress are briefly raised again when Sir Michael Redgrave, apparently an old friend of Brian's whom he has earmarked for the part of Herod, unexpectedly comes to lunch but only, it turns out, in order to arrange the delivery of a large wad of cash to 'Big Freddy', one of Brian's unsavoury contacts, who is blackmailing Redgrave by threatening to 'go to the papers' about his private life. The innocent Robbins is bemused.

> 'What? And tell them Sir Michael's queer? As if they didn't already know?'
> Brian looked at me searchingly, and seemed to be considering whether to continue. 'There are a few "in" jokes about Sir Michael in our circle. "Sir Michael Redgrave, I'll be bound," and "Sir Michael is unable to come to the phone just now, he's all tied up!" Do you understand?'

Robbins gets the point but protests, 'It's a bit rich – I mean, you owe the milkman God knows how much, I've been arrested for non-payment of rates, and here's Big Freddy getting away with blackmail . . .' to which Brian replies: 'Crime pays. Life's not fair. The rich get richer and the poor get poorer – it's all a bleedin' shame.'

So much for Brian's view of life. But what, in fact, was the true life-story of Brian Desmond Hurst? He gives Robbins a version of it at various points, as it becomes increasingly clear that the great religious epic, aka the Box Office Blockbuster, is never going to be made, and Robbins suggests replacing it with another project: the Big Bestseller, the story of Hurst's life as told to Robbins. We hear from Hurst of his father's career as a metal-worker in the Belfast shipyards, where both his father and brother worked on the *Titanic*; and we have his horrific account of his wartime experiences at Gallipoli which must have left a layer of nightmare at the back of his mind for the rest of his life.

As to Hurst's professional career, though pretty well no one I have met has ever heard of him, and some of his claims are hard to credit, between the 1930s and 1960s he was Ireland's most prolific film director, working with many of the great screen actors of his day and with thirty films to prove it, including *Malta Story, Dangerous Moonlight* and *Scrooge* with the inimitable Alastair Sim. After his death he seems to have been totally forgotten, except for a brief moment in 2011 when the Directors' Guild of Great Britain installed a blue plaque to him at the Queen's Film Theatre in his native Belfast.

The flesh-and-blood figure behind these professional facts seems to have been somewhat in the mould of another legendary figure, the late Gerald Hamilton, a 'notorious and wonderfully wicked' old reprobate who was the model for Christopher Isherwood's endearing conman and spy Alfred Norris in *Mr Norris Changes Trains*, and who served prison sentences for bankruptcy, theft, gross indecency and posing a threat to national security. Though Hurst never troubled the courts, he shared some of his friend's underlying characteristics. In his heyday he had been a powerfully magnetic and politically incorrect character. When we encounter him, entering his eighties, he retains all his wit, cunning, gay appetite and preposterous charm.

The Empress of Ireland is a rum story, full of obsession, delusion, wit and hilarity but with pathos never far away – the story of a *folie à deux* which inevitably turns to tragedy as the scales gradually fall from Robbins's eyes and the balance of power between the two of them shifts. Its appeal lies in the Don Quixote-Sancho Panza-like relationship between Hurst and his young amanuensis, with Hurst's impossible dreams and exaggerations seen through the eyes of his somewhat bemused chronicler. He may have been forgotten by the world, but in the pages of this comic masterpiece the unapologetic yet irresistible old rogue lives again, unforgettably.

ANTONY WOOD enjoys impossible projects. He is the founder of the small literary press Angel Books and attempts to translate Pushkin's verse. A selection of his Pushkin translations has just been published by Penguin Classics.

Christopher Robbins's *The Empress of Ireland* (384pp), is now available in a limited and numbered cloth-bound edition of 2,000 copies (subscribers: UK & Eire £17, Overseas £19; non-subscribers: UK & Eire £18.50, Overseas £20.50). All prices include post and packing. Copies may be ordered by post (53 Hoxton Square, London NI 6PB), by phone (020 7033 0258) or via our website www.foxedquarterly.com.

Hazy Memories of Hanging Rock

KATE YOUNG

I have been reading aloud from *Picnic at Hanging Rock* for three hours when my friend touches the window beside her. I do the same; given the blasting air-conditioning, it seems impossible that the glass could be so hot. But it is – we have left behind the breezes of the coast, and the cooling altitude of the mountains. This is the Australian outback, 400 kilometres south-west of Canberra, and it is 44 degrees in the shade. We pull over and step out, and the heat hits us like a wall.

Alongside the heat, it is the sheer emptiness of the country that strikes me; it's miles since we last passed a car. I recall a line I read earlier in the book:

'Except for those people over there with the wagonette we might be the only living creatures in the whole world,' said Edith, airily dismissing the entire animal kingdom at one stroke.

I left Australia on a one-way ticket when I was 21. Somehow, in the intervening decade, I've managed to forget quite how languorous this kind of heat makes me. We drive with the windows down, but the heat is soporific. I think of the girls under the rock, 'overcome by an overpowering lassitude'. My eyes begin to close, and I fumble my way through the next sentences. Despite my discomfort (in truth, because of it), we couldn't have manufactured better conditions for a reading of Joan Lindsay's 1967 Australian classic.

Joan Lindsay, *Picnic at Hanging Rock* (1967)
Vintage · Pb · 208pp · £8.99 · ISBN 9780099577140

On Valentine's Day, 1900, headmistress Mrs Appleyard arranges for her students to enjoy a picnic at Hanging Rock. After lunching on roast chicken and angel cake, and ignoring the fact that all their delicate wristwatches have inexplicably stopped, Miranda, Marion, Irma and Edith set off to climb the Rock in their petticoats and corsets. Hours later, Edith returns alone and in hysterics, and the girls and teachers who remain realize they have lost track of time, and that the maths teacher Greta McGraw has also vanished. They return to the school hours late and in a state of panic.

The community surrounding Hanging Rock is occupied with little else in the weeks following the girls' disappearance. Groups are sent on to the Rock in fruitless searches, and rumours about the fate of the girls begin to circulate. Mike Fitzhubert, recently arrived from England, sets out on a solo mission; he manages to recover an unconscious Irma, but has to be rescued by his friend Alfred, who finds him in a daze at the base of the Rock. At Appleyard College, the usual order has been overturned – parents are removing their daughters from the school, teachers are leaving in droves, and young Sara, who adored Miranda, proves impossible for Mrs Appleyard to handle. The horror of the events on the Rock seems to infect everyone connected with it; there are more unexplained deaths, and the lost hours and days haunt those who survive.

The picnic looms large in my memory. I would happily have sworn that half the book is dedicated to the events of that day. In fact, the focus is on the months that follow, as the aftershocks of the tragedy ripple through the community. The novel is of course about the disappearances, but it is also about the Australian landscape, and a community of people who feel strange in that landscape.

Though my childhood was spent in picket-fence suburbia, I never felt entirely at peace in Australia. More comfortable in the library than on the beach, I built a world among books, and it was in my early years at secondary school that I first discovered *Picnic at Hanging Rock*. Though I found it unsettling, the opening note – Lindsay

speaking directly to us, blurring the line between fact and fiction –
kept me coming back to it:

> Whether *Picnic at Hanging Rock* is fact or fiction, my readers
> must decide for themselves. As the fateful picnic took place in
> the year nineteen hundred, and all the characters who appear in
> this book are long since dead, it hardly seems important.

Much has been written about *Picnic at Hanging Rock* as a reimagining of true events; and in both its opening note and the closing
pseudo-historical document, Lindsay provides an 'explanation' for a
lack of official documentation. For those who don't know the book
or saw only Peter Weir's acclaimed 1975 film adaptation, this may
seem a fair assumption. Within the narrative, Lindsay writes of
rumours:

> As always, in matters of surpassing human interest, those who
> knew nothing whatever either at first or even second hand were
> the most emphatic in expressing their opinions; which are well
> known to have a way of turning into established facts overnight.

Now past my suggestible teenage years, when I was convinced that
the novel must be rooted in fact, I am more comfortable with a story
that leaves its narrative threads in a tangle, rather than determinedly
tying them together. It wasn't until a decade after my first reading
that I discovered the 'final chapter', taken out at the urging of
Lindsay's publishers, who pushed for ambiguity. At least as strange as
the answers readers had been proposing for decades, it is based on
Lindsay's rumoured interest in Spiritualism. It does posit a 'solution'
of sorts, but it is the ending of the first edition – a question mark –
that has stayed with me. It hardly matters, as Lindsay herself said in
an interview: 'If you can draw your own conclusions, that's fine, but
I don't think that it matters. I wrote that book as a sort of atmosphere
of a place, and it was like dropping a stone into the water.'

Joan Lindsay (*née* à Beckett Weigall) attended a girls' school in the state of Victoria in the early twentieth century. Those who wish to draw parallels between Lindsay's childhood and *Picnic at Hanging Rock* make much of the fact that her Melbourne school relocated to Mount Macedon, mere miles from the Rock. However, though she holidayed nearby, this move didn't happen until years after her graduation. During her schooling, she had planned to train as an architect, but she eventually switched to visual art. She married the artist Daryl Lindsay, later director of the National Gallery of Victoria, in 1922. Though she experienced artistic success, she eventually drifted away from it and turned to writing.

In 1966, by then in her late sixties, Lindsay wrote what became her best-known work, finishing it in a matter of weeks. She said that the story came to her in a dream; she told her housekeeper that she could feel the heat of the February sun when she awoke on a cold winter's morning, and then she retreated to the attic to write the dream down. Later, in conversation with her agent, she acknowledged that '*Picnic at Hanging Rock* really was an experience to write, because I was just impossible when I was writing it. I just sort of thought about it all night and in the morning I would go straight up and sit on the floor, papers all around me, and just write like a demon!'

In 1900, when *Picnic at Hanging Rock* is set, Australia was made up of self-governing British colonies and indigenous Australian communities. In 1966, the year before the book's publication, Australia's infamous White Australia Policy was dismantled, though it wasn't until 1973 that legislation against overtly racist policies was passed. Though ostensibly a work of historical fiction, *Picnic at Hanging Rock* has much to say about the complex relationship white Australians have with their country and about the very notion of what it is to be 'Australian'.

Colonial rule hangs heavily over the narrative. In this telling of a horrific (albeit fictional) event it is impossible to ignore the fact that the original custodians of the land, the Dja Dja Wurrung, Wurundjeri and Taungurong people, suffered generations of violence in the shadow of Hanging Rock. Some contracted smallpox, others were murdered by British settlers, those left were moved on to a reserve. Tens of thousands of years of local history were forcibly erased in a century, and the voices of these communities are entirely absent from this narrative, and many others.

Instead, *Picnic at Hanging Rock* views the mystery through the lens of first- and second-generation Australians, English migrants making their home in a harsh and unfamiliar environment. There are those who are unwavering in their wish to recreate a version of England – Mrs Appleyard attempts to operate an English girls' school in the Australian bush. Yet as we follow her pupils, dressed in white muslin and layers of petticoats, making their way through waist-high bracken on Hanging Rock, it is clear that they don't fit into the landscape:

> Insulated from natural contacts with earth, air and sunlight, by corsets pressing on the solar plexus, by voluminous petticoats, cotton stockings and kid boots, the drowsy well-fed girls lounging in the shade were no more a part of their environment than figures in a photograph album, arbitrarily posed against a backcloth of cork rocks and cardboard trees.

There are others who embrace the harsh reality of life in Australia. Mike Fitzhubert, forced to sleep on the ground beneath the Rock the night before he finds Irma, remembers a comfortable evening on the French Riviera, on a picnic rug, in the company of his fellow undergraduates. He feels far from home, and yet he falls irrevocably in love with Australia, with the harsh land, with the opposite of familiarity.

In essence, the novel explores the inescapable discord faced when recreating a set of cultural norms within an uncontrollable and misunderstood environment. As a teenager, it was the girls from Appleyard College I was most fascinated by. Nowadays, I am drawn to Mike, to his desire to become part of Australia without disrupting the natural order of the land, inserting himself into the landscape, rather than changing it to fit him.

Back in the car, like Mrs Appleyard's girls, we're travelling with a bottle of homemade lemonade beside us. It's perfect in the heat, flavoured with ingredients we picked from my friend's garden.

Lemonade
5 lemons (zest and juice)
12 lemon verbena leaves
Rosemary stalk
150g caster sugar
To serve
Lemon verbena leaves
Ice
One bottle sparkling water

Martin Yeoman

Pour the lemon juice, zest, herbs and sugar into a saucepan. Bring to a simmer and reduce until viscous. Cool, and strain into a bottle. Serve with lemon verbena, ice and sparkling water.

Reading of how at peace Mike feels in Australia, I'm struck by a feeling of homesickness, not, ironically, for Australia, but for England; grey winter mornings, bustling streets and changing seasons. Australia is the place I come from, but England is my home.

KATE YOUNG is an award-winning writer and cook. She is the author of *The Little Library Cookbook* and *The Little Library Year*, cookbooks which take inspiration from literature.

Simply Delicious

CLIVE UNGER-HAMILTON

The food writer Theodora FitzGibbon was a late beginner, professionally speaking. Born Theodora Rosling in 1916 she received a cosmopolitan education, travelling widely in Europe and Asia with her Irish father Adam, a naval officer and bon viveur afflicted with wanderlust as well as a wandering eye. Theodora had a number of siblings conceived on the wrong side of the blanket. He also introduced his daughter to the delights of whiskey and cigars at a perilously early age. Later, in her teens, she began to forge a career as an actress on tour and in the West End, while her imperious good looks also helped her find work as a fashion model for some of the best-known couturiers of the day. (An old wartime film called *Freedom Radio*, about German resistance to the Nazi regime within the Third Reich, features the young Theodora Rosling in a cameo part, and is a rattling good yarn into the bargain if you're lucky enough to find it.) It was not until she was in her mid-thirties that she wrote her first cookery book but she went on to produce at least two dozen more.

It is a sad and to me inexplicable fact that even in her own lifetime much of Theodora's work was eclipsed by that of her contemporaries Elizabeth David and Jane Grigson. Her output was impressive, especially the *A Taste of . . .* books, a series she devised with her publisher Dent, starting with Ireland as the first title in 1968.

The concept proved a winner, with recipes, history and anecdotes on one page and wonderful black-and-white photos – many of them

---

Theodora FitzGibbon, *A Taste of Paris, in Food and Pictures* (1974), is out of print but we can obtain second-hand copies.

well over a century old – on the facing page. In *A Taste of Paris* (1974),
for example, the sixth in the series,
gigot au pastis is accompanied by a
picture of the semi-comatose Verlaine
somewhere in Montparnasse with a
generous half-pint of absinthe on
the table in front of him. Finding the
illustrations for the books in the
series, incidentally, was the work of
Theodora's second husband George
Morrison, whom she married in 1960 after divorcing the Irish-
American writer Constantine FitzGibbon.

Coq au vin was the first dish I cooked from *A Taste of Paris* and
perhaps my first serious attempt at French cuisine. It's not difficult:
braising meat is a relatively easy and forgiving process for a beginner.
I used to follow that with Theodora's *parfait au chocolat*, simplicity
itself if you follow her instructions to the letter and a glutton's
delight. So I owe *A Taste of Paris* an enormous debt for initiating me
into the rudiments and refinements of French cooking, though there
was another influence that was to prove equally strong in time.

Traiteurs are to be found all over France, often as part of a butcher's
shop or *charcuterie*. They sell cooked dishes ready for the lazy gourmet
to heat through at home: duck *à l'orange*, *blanquette de veau*, ham with
Madeira sauce and a hundred other delights. The best cook I ever knew
was Annie Roget, married to Pierre whose butcher's shop was across
the road from where we lived in Paris near the Bastille. Each morning
she prepared the most wonderful dishes for lunch that only cost a few
francs per portion: in the afternoon she would often have to look after
the butcher's shop alone while her husband could be found slumped
in a Verlaine-like stupor in front of one of his carcasses after a liquid
lunch at the bar next door.

There was also a little bistro round the corner in the rue Keller, an old-fashioned eating-house (very similar, incidentally, to the one facing Theodora's recipe for *blanquette de veau* with its frowsy workmen posed on classic café chairs), whose regular customers kept their napkins in numbered pigeon-holes by the door and whose mouth-watering three-course lunches were renowned throughout the neighbourhood. Every morning as I stared out of my attic window I would see the *patron* trotting off to market with his shopping-basket on wheels. Braised rabbit with prunes was a favourite in the rue Keller and Theodora's recipe hits the spot precisely, though it should be remembered that in France plump and tender farmed animals are used rather than their lean, athletic and wild cousins that we cook in England.

When I first went to live in Paris entertaining friends was a little daunting. Our apartment remained a building site for almost a year, but we enjoyed the hospitality of our friend Pépo who had a vast one-roomed studio all to himself across the courtyard. Dinners there were enormous fun, though our shopping had to be carefully planned – as yours would be too if you had to carry it up ninety-seven stairs. Sometimes we'd have a rest on the way up and put the shopping down, especially if it had bottles in it.

Theodora's *pot-au-feu* proved an infinitely expandable dish that could feed up to a dozen friends on a Saturday night. (The author cannily includes the advice to throw away the vegetables used in cooking and add fresh ones half an hour or so before serving.) The only problem *chez Pépo* was the WC, which was not in a room by itself but right next to the dining-table, peeping coyly out from behind a potted plant, ignored at first but eventually used by everybody.

Although *A Taste of Paris* is a working cookbook, it has some real rarities among the more traditional classic fare: its author casts a wide net and expresses her determination not to limit her attention to the flashy showpieces of *haute cuisine*. Only this afternoon while I was writing this my wife picked the book up and baked a batch of *petits marcellins*, crunchy little almond pies with rum in the pastry and cointreau in the filling, the like of which I've never tasted before. Theodora's formula for a foolproof *pain de campagne* is another godsend (and the perfect vehicle for mopping up the juices of the Marquise de Valromey's *civet de lièvre*, my own personal favourite in the collection).

Recipes apart, the book's chief delight lies in those pictures which linger in the mind. An image of the immortal Sarah Bernhardt snatching forty winks in the coffin in which she habitually slept is not easily forgotten. Another is a vividly evocative sepia photo *circa* 1882 of a working girl's bed-sitting room heated by a simple coke stove, with a pot on top which supplied her hot water and was used to cook her nightly dinners. According to the first volume of her autobiography, when Theodora arrived in Paris as a young actress in 1938 and met the first great love of her life, the artist and photographer Peter Rose Pulham, they seem to have lived in a very similar room with very similar facilities. Money was short and food was prepared on a home-made arrangement of wire in the fireplace. But it was there that she began seriously to learn to cook.

One of her first successes was braised beef and carrots (*boeuf à la mode*) for which her recipe is included in the book and which I served up for a wedding breakfast at a Paris artist's studio in 1989. This is a dish better eaten cold, and since I was doubling as best man for the occasion it seemed ideal. To serve it up with sautéed potatoes I had the unsolicited assistance of a small boy, the bride's son, and with his over-enthusiastic help it was but a matter of minutes before the gauze curtains at the window caught fire. Flames were soon dancing up to the ceiling and only the miraculous arrival of the fire brigade prevented the wedding from morphing into a funeral.

Eventually we all sat down round a rather damp table and I sliced up the shining log of beef and carrots in its golden jelly but the fun had gone from the celebration. I was no longer the best man, I was in disgrace, and I have never felt tempted to cook *boeuf à la mode* again.

CLIVE UNGER-HAMILTON worked in restaurants in London and France before he and his wife opened the first fish-and-chip shop in Paris in 1987.

An Outsider in Tregonissey

ANNABEL WALKER

When I was a child growing up in Devon, I held a rather dim view of
Cornwall. The landscape of claypits and roadside caffs glimpsed from
the car en route to the beach seemed bleak. It wasn't that I found the
far west boring, simply that my interest was unconnected to twentieth-
century realities and focused instead on the romance of Daphne
du Maurier's historical novels. If I found the modern county prosaic,
I could bury myself in tales of dashing French sailors or murderous
smugglers on the high moors. Later, John Betjeman's *Summoned by
Bells* alerted me to less flamboyant but equally seductive charms. Still,
I was in the realm of romantic sentiment, aware that most lives in the
county were not as enchanted as that of a privileged young boy on
holiday from Highgate in the early twentieth century.

In the years that saw Betjeman taking exciting train journeys from
London to Wadebridge, Alfred Leslie Rowse, later to become an eminent academic and historian, was living in rather different circumstances
a few miles to the south in the village of Tregonissey, on the outskirts
of St Austell. The son of a clayworker, he spent his entire life up to the
age of 18 in this small community. His only experience of train travel
was the annual Sunday School outing to the sea at Pentewan, three
miles away, in china clay rail trucks that had been specially cleaned for
the occasion. Like Betjeman, he later wrote vividly about his childhood
and the resulting memoir was published in 1942.

There will be readers who find *A Cornish Childhood* too rooted in

---

A. L. Rowse, *A Cornish Childhood* (1942), is out of print but we can obtain
second-hand copies.

the egotism for which A. L. Rowse was well-known, or uncomfortably tinged with disdain for others – he dishes out verdicts such as 'vapid', 'deplorable' and 'puerile' with seeming equanimity and is unafraid of making dismissive generalizations about 'the people'. At a distance of almost eighty years from publication, I mostly feel fairly forgiving towards such comments, amused rather than outraged and prepared to overlook them since his outspokenness seems so obviously a product of his particular circumstances.

The circumstances are these: an unusually bright boy is born in 1903 into a family of modest means whose world is circumscribed by village and work. Life, as Rowse wrote later, proceeded 'along very well-worn ruts'. Of course, this was still common in the early twentieth century, particularly in remote parts of the country. We know that most people necessarily lived parochial, often difficult and wretched lives and that many either could not or did not read or write (elementary schooling had become compulsory only thirty years earlier), did not travel, rarely took holidays or met people from beyond their own familiar territory.

The bare historical facts are known – but written, highly readable accounts of the real experiences of such a community are rare. How could they be otherwise, since those communities produced few people with the skills and inclination to organize their memories into book form?

In this young boy, however, Tregonissey had a future chronicler. From the outset Rowse seems to have had a deep interest in learning, an innate sense of history and a facility with words. He is keenly sensitive to emotion, place and aesthetics. He seeks out books, teachers, mentors; he spends hours immersed in study. All this sets him apart; he is an outsider and an observer. Also, happily for future readers, he has a phenomenal memory. What a combination!

Written when Rowse was in his late thirties after years of ill-health and life-threatening illness, the book is primarily an affectionate and nostalgic description of his Cornish childhood – unlike the difficulties he had when composing books on history and politics, he commented in the Preface, this book 'was there waiting to write itself'. Woven throughout his account, however, is an inextricable sub-theme, like a continuous thread in a piece of cloth, a couple of shades deeper than all the others: the resentment clearly still burning in him at being under-appreciated by his family and forced to struggle at every step on the way to becoming first a scholar and then an academic. 'I admit that I was exceedingly inquisitive,' he writes,

> devoured by an insatiable desire to know and in every direction . . . So a technique of dealing with me was developed from my earliest years. My questions were unanswered; the more I asked the less satisfaction I got; I was told on every hand: 'Little boys should be seen and not heard' . . .
>
> I grant that I must have been an altogether too knowing little boy, or would have been if the questions had been answered – if they had been capable of answering them. But this process of stubbing every shoot of confidence on the part of a naturally sanguine and vivacious temperament had all sorts of unforeseen consequences, some of them detrimental to happiness. For one thing, this repressive, discouraged youth drove me in upon myself and made me excessively ambitious . . .

You can see how that prickly, provocative and outspoken character developed.

He sought affirmation from his teachers, whether in school or at church where he was a chorister, found few friends among other children and had no like-minded relatives – though he enjoyed spending time with his spirited great-aunt and uncle, who read to each other from Dickens. As a very young child he seems to have noticed that the dialect his family spoke was not 'correct' and felt acute shame if anyone drew attention to his using it. He must have made a determined effort to shed it because he says that he became unable to speak it for many years – understandable at a time when many of his peers at Oxford would no doubt have judged him for having a regional accent and a vocabulary to match. By the time the book was published, however, he was secure enough to enjoy the dialect and is adept at reproducing it accurately on the page.

Tregonissey, 1912 (Francis Frith Collection)

Rowse compensates for the perceived lack of family support by channelling his emotions into a love of his native county and all that that encompassed: the physical contours of the place, its history and its people. He writes with such vivid recall that you almost feel the road dust in your nostrils and hear the voices of the carters calling to their horses on the way from the claypits to the town. You experience his wariness of the older boys at primary school wielding stones, his awe-struck fascination during a visit to the unoccupied 'big house' where his grandparents were employed, and his terror while reading the frightening passages of *Jane Eyre* under the bedclothes. He loves trips to the coast but is scared of the sea (no one goes in the water on the Sunday School outing); his experience of the First World War is mostly confined to rumours and a depopulated neighbourhood; he is as familiar with the columns of the *Cape Times* as with those of the local paper, because so many former miners seek their fortunes in South Africa, but is overcome when once invited to dine at the Rectory.

He describes a society of rituals and restraints, hard work and heavy responsibilities. His mother and father were respectably poor, with no spare cash and strict rules: no liquor in the house, best clothes and church (not chapel) on Sundays, many duties on other days including cleaning scales and weights in the shop his mother ran, measuring out flour and lamp oil for customers, selling oranges round the village and chopping sticks on Saturdays. He found such work demeaning and vexatious, convinced 'that *my* work, my reading and writing, was infinitely more important', and often fell into 'a sullen ill-temper' (for which he is unapologetic).

He couldn't know, and didn't intuit then, how precarious a life of hard-working respectability was, nor what his parents might feel, or deny themselves. By the time he writes the book, however, he understands that

> something in my father had been deeply hurt by the circumstances of his early family life; recollections of the past, though they began well, brought up associations which gave him acute pain. He was a man of simple texture, upright, hard-working, honourable, of a distinctly Puritan cast of character; but he was uneducated, unintrospective, unsubtle and naturally incapable . . . of seeing himself and his environment objectively, of locating the pain, diagnosing it and gaining relief from it by self-expression.

While he often immersed himself in the history and romance of far-flung places, Rowse himself barely travelled even within Cornwall during his childhood. The places he knew beyond his village were of necessity within easy reach by foot or in the family donkey-cart and he seems not to have considered going for long walks until, as a teenager, he was introduced to the idea by a fellow choir member. They walked to St Blazey, then through Prideaux Woods to the village of Luxulyan. 'It might have been the Tyrol,' he wrote, 'it was so strangely beautiful, and for all I knew that there was such country within half a dozen miles of the place where I was born and had lived all my days.'

In 1973, after a career in academia during which he became an authority on the Tudor period and a prolific author (interrupted by several unsuccessful attempts in the 1930s to become a Member of Parliament for Penryn and Falmouth), A. L. Rowse retired to Trenarren House, about three miles south of Tregonissey. By the time he died in 1997, the Eden Project was being planned in a claypit close to that walk he took to Luxulyan, and Tregonissey had long since been absorbed into the northern suburbs of St Austell. His long life spanned many changes in his beloved county but it's easy to forget all those when you become absorbed in this vivid evocation of an unusual childhood.

ANNABEL WALKER has changed her mind about Cornwall.

Partying down at the Palace

MICK HERRON

Books have their own sweet spot. Some arrive too late (the window for *The Catcher in the Rye* is narrow; read it after the age of 16, and chances are you'll notice that it's a shallow, narcissistic whine) and some too soon: I was put off the whole of Russian literature by too early an encounter with Alexander Solzhenitsyn. But others have perfect pitch and perfect timing, and recalling your first encounter is like remembering a summer day from your teens. They're the books that lodge in your heart while it's still wide open, and they become the platform for the reading you'll do ever after.

I read enough at that age to have a fairly wide platform, even if it's one whose strength I've not often tested in the intervening years. Nobody wants to discover that they're walking on rotting woodwork. But circumstances recently reintroduced me to John Steinbeck's *Sweet Thursday* after a thirty-year gap, and I'm happy to say that, on a rereading, I felt nothing give beneath my feet. All these years later, it still bears weight.

Sweet Thursday, published in 1954, is a sequel to *Cannery Row* (1945). Both are set in the Californian town of Monterey, once a bright and bustling place whose canning industry meant that the locals could always find employment when all else failed, but which in the post-war years – 'when all the pilchards were caught and canned and eaten' – has become a sleepy backwater, no part of which is dozier than Cannery Row itself, where the same few dollars make

John Steinbeck's *Sweet Thursday* (1954) and *Cannery Row* (1945) are both available as Penguin paperbacks at £8.99 and £9.99 respectively.

the same regular journeys between saloon and grocery and brothel, everyone owes money to somebody else, and nobody's really keeping score.

The Row's main citizens are Doc, a marine biologist and natural-born philosopher who runs Western Biological Laboratories, and Mack and the boys, who live in the Palace Flophouse and get by on charm and petty larceny, but dozens of others – cops and barflies, artists and plumbers, bouncers and beach bums – stray on and off the page. Allowing for a few lost to war and other mischances, the same characters populate both books, whose plots, if plots they have, are whisper-thin. In *Cannery Row*, Mack and the boys decide to do something nice for Doc: this turns out to be a party. Unfortunately the party happens when Doc's not around, and ends with his laboratory a mess of shattered glass and broken furniture. Everyone on the Row feels bad about this, and the gloom that settles only shifts when Mack and the boys decide to do something nice for Doc. This turns out to be a party . . .

There's more to *Sweet Thursday*, but not much – a new girl called Suzy arrives in town, Doc falls for her, and everyone does their best to make sure romance blossoms, which creates more obstacles than it removes. That 'new girl' in this context means 'hooker', adding a layer of grim realism – Steinbeck knew about poverty, and the narrow choices it enforces – but *Sweet Thursday* takes place in a different world to *The Grapes of Wrath*, and Suzy's a sex worker in the same way that the guys in *Guys and Dolls* were gangsters. People get killed, sure, but nobody actually gets hurt. (Damon Runyon's *On Broadway* is another of the planks in my platform.)

There's sadness aplenty in both books, and an awareness that some lives are damaged beyond repair, but it's a sadness that offers itself up for consolation, to be found in the company of fellow human beings, and in drink, and sex, and riotous behaviour. These books celebrate the rackety nature of life, and as such are far bigger than their slim spines suggest.

And if plot is largely absent, that's not to say that there's not plenty of incident. An unlucky horoscope reading dooms Hazel, one of Mack's boys, to become President of the United States; luckily, this turns out to be inaccurate. A couple living in a boiler in a vacant lot make a decent enough home out of it, though their bid for domesticity breaks down with an attempt to put up curtains in the windowless cavity. Frogs are hunted; fights are fought. A neighbouring town, Pacific Grove, descends into civil war when a local philanthropist gifts it two roque courts, roque being 'a complicated kind of croquet'. Fauna, the owner – previously a mission worker called Flora – pins gold stars on the wall of the Bear Flag brothel, one for each of 'her girls' who marries well: 'My young ladies go places.' And Mack and the boys conspire to keep the grocery's new owner from realizing that he also now owns the Palace Flophouse by raffling it and ensuring that Doc holds the winning ticket, a conspiracy marred only by their failure to realize that their previous landlord had deeded them the property before leaving town. ('Doc, would you do me the favor?' Mack asks. 'Don't tell the boys.')

As with other Steinbeck novels, then, one of the delights of both books is that they're filled with characters more usually found in the margins: they're bit-part players elevated to leading roles because their author, like most sensible readers, would rather hang out with sinners than saints. Not that the doings of Mack and the boys are especially venal. The language is gently bowdlerized ('Why don't you take a flying fuggut the moon?' one character invites another), while the parameters of the dishonesty on display are carefully adjusted to take account of who its victims might be. And in their ready acceptance of the blows life delivers, the denizens of Cannery Row acquire a tattered grace that, in the right light, resembles heroism.

This is a necessary virtue: if life isn't brutal on Cannery Row, it can sometimes be harsh. Suicide and sadness are part of the human comedy, and frog-hunting is as sacred a ritual as anything organized religion has to offer. The characters are as apt to express their love for each other as they are to pile into a fist-fight but they know that a good fist-fight is worth travelling miles for. That people are poor or homeless or have sex for money does not render them unworthy of respect, and the kindness of the community holds all in its embrace.

Steinbeck, who wrote a version of the tales of King Arthur, recognized honour when he found it, and lays it out here in shop-soiled form. And none of his knights are more honourable than Doc, because *Sweet Thursday* is also an elegy, and Doc is based on Steinbeck's great friend and scientific mentor Ed Ricketts, who was alive when *Cannery Row* was written but who died when his car was hit by a train on a level crossing. If a rock-and-roll death is a plane crash, a train wreck is a truly literary departure. So the affection that seeps out of the novel has its roots in a real-world love; Steinbeck was allowing a happy ending, a continuation, for a friend.

And en route to that ending there are wonderful comic moments, one of the set pieces being *Sweet Thursday*'s fancy dress party. (There are a lot of parties; these people know how to have fun.) This particular event has two aims; to allow Doc to end up with the winning ticket in the Palace Flophouse raffle, and to ensure that he and Suzy realize they are made for each other. To this end, Mack and the boys bribe a child dressed as Eros – 'I'm Cupid, God of Love, and I draw a bead on unsuspecting hearts' – to target the happy couple. The conversation, a masterpiece of comic timing and phrasing, is one I've often recalled when contemplating how to construct dialogue:

'I want thirty-five cents,' said Johnny.
  'What!'
  'If I don't get thirty-five cents I'll tell.'
  'Mack,' said Whitey No. 2, 'this here kid's jumped the price.'
  'Give it to him,' said Mack. 'I'll flip him double or nothing later.'
  'Not with that two-headed nickel you won't,' said Johnny.

'Seems like kids got no respect for their elders nowadays,' Eddie observed. 'If I ever said that, my old man would of clobbered me.'

'Maybe your old man wasn't rigging no raffle,' said Johnny.

Whitey No. 1 said, 'This kid ain't honest. You know where bad kids go, Johnny?'

'I sure do, and I been there,' said Johnny.

'Give him the thirty-five cents,' said Mack.

That's more or less seared into my mind, but in rereading both books, I found that every other page I had an awareness of what was coming next: not simply a scene or an event, but an actual phrase or sentence. And I was right every time. These novels are embedded in my heart.

So why did *Sweet Thursday*, and *Cannery Row* too, land so hard? Perhaps because it was the first time I'd met such people in books. I've always had a strong romantic streak, but I was probably more attuned to Jane Austen characters than to these beautifully rendered lowlifes: the jobless, the dreamers, the drinkers. I don't know if these books made me want to be a writer, but they certainly made the life of a shiftless layabout seem attractive, and what are novels for, if not to open our eyes to the alternative lives on offer? So in honour of Doc, Mack, Suzy and the rest, I'm calling it a day now, at 11.23 in the morning. And I'm going to drink beer in the sunshine.

MICK HERRON's fictional spies – the Slow Horses – wouldn't look out of place in the Palace Flophouse. But Mick himself lives in Oxford and has no plans to raffle his home any time soon.

These Fragments

JON WOOLCOTT

'Deepdene, The Grange, Little Ridge, Sturton Hall . . .' Visitors to
the V&A's landmark 1974 exhibition 'The Destruction of the
Country House' would have heard a recorded voice intoning the
names of houses that had disappeared in previous decades. This voice
belonged to John Harris, the architectural historian, and co-curator
of the exhibition.

I've always loved ruins and vanished buildings. If you share that
interest, and many don't, finding a fellow obsessive is wonderful. My
fascination had lasted decades before I came across Harris's book *No
Voice from the Hall* (1998) and found a kindred spirit. Subtitled *Early
Memories of a Country House Snooper*, it describes his teenage expeditions hitch-hiking across England – mostly – in search of derelict
great houses in the aftermath of the Second World War.

*

A history class during my first year at grammar school in the late
1970s: a warm day in early autumn, the room hotter than it needed
to be. Thirty or so boys, uncomfortable in prickly new uniforms,
seated at old desks in a grey prefabricated 'mobile' classroom, which
smelt fiercely of plastic and rubber. We were doing local history and
weren't especially interested, but the lesson was bearable because our
school was in Salisbury and history there was palpable: the famous
cathedral spire loomed over the school; Old Sarum, the hill fort to

---

John Harris, *No Voice from the Hall: Early Memories of a Country House Snooper*
(1998), is out of print but we can obtain second-hand copies.

the north, was visible from everywhere in this valley town; and Stonehenge lay a few miles away.

Now our teacher, Mr Pemberton, was talking about Clarendon Palace. I had never heard of it. A retreat for monarchs, it boasted a Great Hall, wine cellars, chapel, courtyard, gardens. The Constitutions of Clarendon, introducing new legal practices, had been enacted there by Henry II. As an aside, in words I can remember precisely from that lesson forty years ago, we were told that the palace 'now lay derelict in woods beyond Laverstock'. I looked around – my classmates were unmoved, the sportier ones gazing through smeary windows towards the cricket nets. But I was transfixed. I imagined a huge, ornate building, a wide frontage and steps up to a massive blank doorway, in near darkness under the thick canopy, secluded, undisturbed. The depth of my obsession has never diminished.

On the other side of a poorly negotiated adolescence I took my mother, always a woman keen for adventure, on a walk to find the palace. An Ordinance Survey map led us up downland and along a chalky path to an isolated cottage. Just beyond, hidden in tall grass and brambles, I spotted a small square sign headed 'Ministry of Works' that announced an archaeological site. We pushed through the undergrowth; trees gathered overhead. Suddenly a section of thick flint wall loomed above us. This was it.

In the green darkness my heart thumped. The find was confirmed by a nineteenth-century plaque commemorating the Constitutions of Clarendon – Mr Pemberton would have approved. We roamed around. Among tree roots we stumbled over massive bases of pillars – the Great Hall, surely. Beyond, the ground fell away steeply. Behind the high wall a set of crumbling steps led down to a roofless chamber with flint walls. It was unspeakably thrilling. I have since visited many ruins, follies and grottoes – all are wonderful, but few have produced that first pure rush of discovery.

John Harris was born in 1931 and says, matter of factly, that his parents 'couldn't cope' with him. They ended his schooling when he was 14 and found him employment at Heal's on Tottenham Court Road. It did not last. A very long lunch break taken volunteering at the British Museum got him the sack. Escape from the mundane lay in spending days with his 'Uncle' Sid, whose huge red bulbous nose earned him the nickname Snozzle. Snozzle had been a shepherd, knew the works of the Victorian writer and nature-mystic Richard Jefferies intimately, and would lie on ancient earthworks to commune with the earth's spirits. He was also an accomplished fisherman and Harris became one too. Angling in remote spots, sometimes in the lakes of large estates, gave the young man a taste for exploring the houses' dereliction.

Following his spell at Heal's, the dole came to his rescue, giving him just enough money to fuel his interest, criss-crossing the country and staying at youth hostels, visiting abandoned houses. Later, with steadier employment, he travelled with friends and colleagues. Between 1946 and 1960 he visited more than 200 houses. The buildings were dangerous to poke about in, especially when alone, full of unstable staircases, collapsed roofs, and floors where a misstep could result in disaster.

War had been unkind to them. No other country, says Harris, subjected its great houses to the ignominy of occupation by regiments, requisition for hospitals and schools, or temporary refuge for evacuees. This was a product of the Dunkirk Spirit – the complete mobilization of the country. Nissen huts, training courses and firing-ranges filled the parks. Rolls House in Essex had eighteen different regiments stationed there during the war – staircases were axed for firewood, a portrait of Emma Harvey was used as a dart-board and defaced with a moustache. The Nazis had a go there too – a V1 fell nearby, and the blast blew off part of the roof.

Even after the depredations of occupation, many of these houses were not physically threatened but were 'simply and sadly unwanted'. The rate of destruction was astonishing – in 1955 one great house vanished every two and a half days.

Amid the ruination Harris was a prowler, a trespasser. He describes a typical approach to an abandoned house and gives some tips to the would-be uninvited visitor. Look casual, not furtive; broken windows and mild vandalism are 'good signs' that the house is probably unoccupied and unsecured. 'There is blankness in its glassy stare,' he says, conjuring brilliantly the atmosphere of ruins. Sometimes he employed ruses to gain access, assuming the identity of a fictitious aristocrat, or of a second cousin from abroad, on occasion coming close to being found out.

Harris's prose has an echo of Pevsner, but it's warmer, less emphatic. The influence is not surprising – Harris worked for Pevsner, and while he regarded him as a mentor and a spur they disagreed over methods, and Harris was sacked again. But they remained in contact and during a second stint Harris worked on the Lincolnshire edition of the *Buildings*

The Orangery, Fairford Park, Gloucestershire

of England series. Despite his occasional briskness – in one sentence an aristo is summarily dispatched ('he bloodily shot himself with a revolver in 1931') – Harris always has feeling for his real subjects, the buildings themselves, and their pain.

> The traveller through England after 1945 journeyed in a dream-like landscape, so many empty houses standing forlornly in their parks, all in a vacuum, awaiting the return of their owners to decide their ultimate fate.

His concern is with the mansions and the ruling classes finally down on their luck, but among the decrepitude Harris found others who had taken possession, often coming across 'old-school tramps' living in portions of these vast abandoned houses.

The book's charm lies not only in its mournful subject but in its many idiosyncrasies. Harris is surprisingly saucy, and not just in his chapter headings ('Clock Trouble or "Old Testicle"', 'Into the Arms of the Tart next door'). At one point he writes: 'I will not comment upon the naked lady who met me at the door of a Wolds farmhouse, or the consequences' and 'rural places . . . seemed to retain certain of the primal passions found in characters from Hardy's novels'.

He is keenly aware of the oddity of his mission and the strangeness of what he finds – a room in a mansion filled with a potato harvest, a long dead dog in a bathtub. There are scenes of strange co-incidence and at times he feels haunted by presences. A sense of the romantic or gothic is never far away. Climbing over a gate into the then dilapidated but now magnificently restored gardens at Painshill, Surrey, close to where traffic thunders by on the A3, he encounters a ruined tower, which puts him in mind of Transylvania and vampires. He is attuned to the mysterious atmosphere of these places, and delights in the improbable.

This atmosphere, the indecipherable feeling of a ruin, is what attracts those of us who pick through their fragments. In the early years of this century, after years away, I returned to work in Salisbury. I fell in love, and on one of our early dates I took my future wife to find the ruins of Clarendon. It was an enormously promising sign that she took to the idea with something approaching enthusiasm.

It was early summer. Starting from the village of Pitton we walked west towards Salisbury, across open fields and into the densely for-ested Clarendon Park. Not having approached the ruin from this direction before, I stopped frequently to peer into the woodland, looking for tell-tale signs – a low wall, a dark shadow. Unexpectedly the trees gave way to a huge clearing, and with a start I saw the pal-ace standing alone in the open. It was inestimably reduced. We approached through the long grass. I found it difficult to reconcile it with my memory. Doubt and mystery had been banished; the pal-ace's skeleton was exposed to the July sky. The tall molar-shaped section of wall, its inscription intact, was impressive still, but less so than when shrouded in trees. A short section of narrow-gauge railway was now visible among the ruins, a relic of 1930s excavations. The steep slope my mother and I had encountered beyond the ruin was now revealed as the grassy remains of terraced gardens.

We read the new information signs. We were not alone – an archaeologist working close to the large wall was happy to take a short break to chat. I learnt that the clearance had taken place just a few years before. I wondered then and wonder now about my reaction. Surely this was better, to expose the ruin, to tell its story, rather than hiding it away in the forest as my own snobbish conceit?

Harris has done more than almost any other single person alive to halt the decline of these buildings. Among many projects he was instrumental in the rehabilitation of the gardens and follies at Painshill, with its vampiric tower. Here's the rub for him, and for me: once restored, a place loses its romantic appeal. Maybe we're no better than Grand Tourists on a budget, drawn by visions of ivy-covered ruins in Renaissance-style landscapes. But the feeling remains, nonetheless. When T. S. Eliot wrote 'These fragments I have shored against my ruins' he meant that the great works of world literature had given him strength and purpose: for me, and I suspect for Harris too, it is ruins themselves that give us a glimpse of deeper meaning. Knowing that time and nature take back our efforts is some comfort in difficult times: *No Voice from the Hall* is, above all, strangely optimistic.

JON WOOLCOTT works for the publisher Little Toller. He is writing a book about the hidden and radical histories of the south of England.

On the Shoulders of Giants

ANDREW JOYNES

What we used to call 'the old road' runs beside an ancient waterway that links the English Channel with the Sussex Weald. A thousand years ago one of the companions of the Conqueror fortified a bluff above the river, and sixty years ago the ruined walls of the Norman castle marked the beginning of a bicycle journey that my brother and I made each summer weekend to a grass-runwayed airfield at the river mouth.

We would race past a Saxon church, its western hindquarters sunk into the hillside, a kindly beast emerging from its lair. We would teeter in slow motion beside the dark timbers of a medieval bridge. And by the time we dismounted to wheel our bicycles across the main road beneath the glass escarpment of a public school's immense chapel, we would be looking seawards to the windsock of the airfield and skywards for the light aircraft – Tiger Moths, Chipmunks, Dragon Rapides – which were the objects of our plane-spotting pilgrimage.

I am reminded of those sunlit days, and of the 'whooshpering' sound of the canvas wings as the aircraft swept in above us, whenever I take down my copy of T. H. White's *England Have My Bones* (1936). It is a book for browsing, for it takes the form of a journal which White kept through four seasons in 1934–5, the year he took flying lessons at a small airfield in the middle of England. Flying was his main summer activity; he spent the spring fishing for salmon in

---

T. H. White, *England Have My Bones* (1936), is out of print but we can obtain second-hand copies.

Scotland; the autumn rough shooting; the winter riding to hounds. The journal also contains delightful passages about entirely random matters. He writes about the grass snakes which he keeps loose in his study; about the surging kick of the super-charger on the engine of his Bentley; and about the effects of weather on mood: 'If your senses become sharpened it generally means wet. Thus country people redouble their efforts at harvest if they can hear distant railways . . .'

Each of his journal entries can be savoured like a poem. Those that deal with flying were written after each lesson and are full of detailed notes. Sometimes the notes are exultant: 'I like gliding turns; theoretically I rather like spins . . .' Sometimes they are contrite: 'This was a sad instructive lesson, but well worth having I suppose . . .' They are both witty and surreal, and they uphold the aphorism of White's alter ego in his most celebrated work *The Once and Future King*: 'The best thing for being sad', said Merlyn, 'is to learn something . . .' Such was the earnest accumulation of learning heaped up in these journal entries that one senses White must have been very sad indeed at this time.

White's reasons for taking flying lessons were various. There was a competitive instinct, in that a national newspaper was offering to pay the tuition expenses of any pupil at an English airfield deemed most promising by his flying instructor – evidence of growing public concern about Britain's lack of preparedness for any future air war with Germany. Exhibitionism also played its part, because the image of the daring aviator coincided with a projection of dandyism which White liked to cultivate at the time. It meshed with the overall impression of a Bentley-driving, sharp-shooting, fly-tying, hard-riding country gentleman with literary tastes: a useful persona for a freelance writer to convey to the class-conscious magazine editors of the time.

But there were deeper psychological reasons. He was about to leave his job as a teacher at Stowe School in Buckinghamshire and was living in a cottage nearby with the intention of what today might be called 'finding himself'. He may well have been anxious about the self that he would discover. Helen Macdonald's recent *H is for Hawk* draws heavily on White's exquisite monograph *The Goshawk*. She suggests its author channelled a tortured sexuality – of which he was becoming increasingly aware in the 1930s when he was undergoing psychoanalysis – into a complex devotional relationship with a bird of prey, a creature for whom killing is instinctive and without guilt. Macdonald affectionately calls him 'Mr White', and in her book he becomes a ghostly mentoring presence as she herself trains a goshawk and comes to terms with her grief at the death of her father.

A few days after enrolling on the flying course White acknow-ledges, 'I have always been a coward: afraid of things that hurt, body or soul . . . And now it is flying. I am afraid of aeroplanes. Because I am afraid of things, of being hurt and death, I have to attempt them . . .' The suggestion that confrontation is a cure for cowardice is a dark foreshadowing of Merlyn's aphorism about learning as a cure for sadness.

In a sense White's journal is about fear in every season of the year he chronicles. He is frightened not merely of death and injury, but – more subtly – that he will fail to gain acceptance by the people who are his sporting companions. In the spring he fears he will not be accorded respect by the ghillie who watches him cast over a salmon river; at the autumn pheasant-shoot he worries about not organizing the beaters properly; in the winter he urges his horse over a danger-ous fence to impress the formidable elders of a fox-hunt. And in midsummer the respect he craves is that of his flying instructor: 'I am terrified of Johnny, as everybody is; but with a curious confiding terror . . . I wouldn't trust him with a farthing, a drink or my fiancée, but he could have my heart. It is like this with all good and great people . . .' When, halfway through the course, the instructor lets slip that he has been the most promising student that season, White is ecstatic (it is not clear whether he went on to claim the newspaper's contribution to his expenses).

Gradually, under the instructor's guidance, the pupil gains the ultimate acceptance, that of the flying machine itself. It is time to go solo. In a revealing touch White's journal entry speaks of the

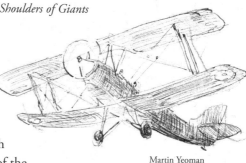

Martin Yeoman

plane and himself in the first person plural – as 'we' – during the final moments of his first solo flight: 'We flattened, flattened, straight, perfect, touching, touching, tail, rumble, still straight, even on the ground, and not a bounce, not a bounce . . .' He then switches to the third person singular in studied nonchalance: 'He had done his solo. He shook hands with himself . . .'

By the end of the summer, with the mechanics of flight mastered, White is beginning to relax and look over the rim of his open cockpit with the eye of a writer. The details he picks out are those of the vanished world of the 1930s. He follows a railway line and overtakes an express train, the smoke pluming from the steam locomotive far below. 'For a few seconds there was a red star, like the sun's reflection from a conservatory roof, but strontium coloured. In fact I was looking down into the furnace of the railway engine's boiler, a door about two feet square, from a height of nearly half a mile . . .' He describes the enormous airship sheds at Cardington, and the pylons at Hatfield, bedecked like chivalric pavilions, round which the competitors in the King's Cup air race flew in their dramatic racing turns. White's flying instructor Johnny came second in the 1934 King's Cup, flying his first heat in a July thunderstorm, and White was there to watch him: 'nor could I give a true picture of the black sky out of which a tiny aeroplane draggled itself, lonely and exhausted. It was something about human splendour . . .'

As I lay on the grassy bank in the sunshine beside the river sixty years ago, I imagined that every plane that passed overhead was the focus of just such a drama. Every take-off, every swing round the airfield above the river and the castle and the Saxon church was special. The pilots may have been carrying out the routine 'circuits and bumps' required of every apprentice flyer – after all, the basic rule of aviation is that take-off is optional, while landing is compulsory – but to the youthful watcher these humdrum exercises had an epic quality.

There was the sound. The thrumming of wires as the plane swooped overhead. The tick of the idling propeller. The shriek of the suspension at the point of touch-down. And then the flatulent surge of the engine striving to become airborne again.

There was also the sight of flying machines whose designs – even in the 1950s – would have been familiar to White at his pre-war airfield. There were biplanes like the Tiger Moth, the lovely successor to the Gipsy Moth on which he learned to fly. And the Dragon Rapide, a passenger biplane whose Art Deco design – tapering wings with curved tips like those of dragonflies – was emblematic of the 1930s. Early each Saturday we bicycled to the aerodrome to watch the departure of the weekly flight to the Channel Islands, when the instruction aircraft suspended their humdrum activities and waited, like courtiers, for the regal passage of the Dragon Rapide into the western sky.

I have always felt there is a yearning, aspirational quality about the sight and sound of light aircraft high in the summer sky; and from time to time I dip into *England Have My Bones* to recall the boyhood romance of watching a world of amateur flying in the 1950s which was not unlike the world of flying in the 1930s.

Between those decades, of course, the nature of mainstream aviation had changed forever. The aviation war of the 1940s which some newspapers had foreseen when White decided to try and win his tuition expenses transformed flying. A year or two ago I had a long conversation with a remarkable man in the East Kent village where I live. Henry had been a Pathfinder pilot during the war, flying Lancaster bombers, and had been shot down over Berlin in 1944. He died in 2018 at the age of 96, and a villager leaving his memorial service was heard to remark, 'We are pygmies on the shoulders of giants . . .'

In his mid-80s Henry took up flying again and went solo in a Piper Cub, one of the standard instruction aircraft of the modern flying club. 'Don't even think about the insurance!' he told me during our conversation. I asked him to describe the difference between piloting a Lancaster during the war and flying a light aircraft today. He thought long and hard, and finally said, 'Well, I suppose the Lancaster was like a combine harvester. The Cub is an autumn leaf . . .'

It was a deft comparison, and one to which the writer T. H. White – helmeted, goggled and gauntleted in his open cockpit – might well have given an aviator's thumbs-up.

When he left the BBC, and a frenzied life as a current affairs producer, ANDREW JOYNES entered a reflective phase of existence. In his writing – as in his reading – he increasingly visits a vintage-stocked cellar of youthful memories of Sussex.

A Long Way from Surrey

SIMON WINDER

Like so many other, reasonably busy individuals I used to think of Christmas as a great opportunity to read a big classic novel. I wrecked the holiday for years with the same repeated, idiotic misunderstanding, struggling to finish *The Golden Bowl* or *The Way We Live Now* or *Daniel Deronda*, until I began to hate the very idea of Christmas reading. But a decade ago I took a decision which has made me happy ever since. At Christmas I would read only short books.

This switch was first achieved when I decided to limit my holiday reading to the four extraordinary little fantasies that H. G. Wells wrote in quick succession, starting in 1894 at a desk in a Sevenoaks boarding-house: *The Time Machine*, *The Island of Doctor Moreau*, *The Invisible Man* and *The War of the Worlds*. When he had finished he had gone from total obscurity to being one of the most famous authors in the world.

The four books are all strikingly brief, but they launched in a seemingly effortless way all the major strands of science fiction and their endless progeny which still choke every bookshop and television screen in ways that Wells would have found both gratifying and alarming.

Three of them are set in various parts of the ancient but sometimes gimcrack country south-west of London with which Wells was very familiar. His attitude to its inhabitants in these novels is somewhat cold: scaring them with the antics of Griffin, the invisible man; kill-

---

H. G. Wells, *The Island of Doctor Moreau* (1896), is out of print but we can obtain second-hand copies.

ing them with poison gas and death rays produced by invading Martians; turning their descendants in the Richmond of 8,000 centuries ahead into lurking, troglodyte Morlocks.

The fourth novel, *The Island of Doctor Moreau* (1896), is the odd one out and is often overlooked. It is very different in tone and is set a long way from Surrey. While the others are more like brief sketches which have been filled in and elaborated on by countless films, sequels and spin-offs over the years, *The Island of Doctor Moreau* is an idea which is fully realized and which only works on the page. It is effectively the transcript of a nightmare, a terrible series of glimpses of depravity, and these cannot really be elaborated on, let alone physically shown in a film, without their fevered, asphyxiating quality being replaced by mere silliness.

The story is told by a highly unfortunate Englishman, Edward Prendick, the sole survivor of a wreck, who has been picked up by a broken-down and seedy trading ship filled with wild animals, ranging in size from rabbits to a puma roaring in its cage. Within a couple of pages his Victorian readers would have been lulled into thinking they knew what they were in for. It was a well-established literary tradition that the Pacific islands tended to create moral weakness and depravity among 'white men' who washed up there. So it is no surprise that the narrator should find on his rescue ship a violent, drunk captain and a weak-willed young man with 'watery grey expressionless eyes' who turns out to have done something furtive and shameful (the implication is gay) back in London, forcing him to wander in eternal exile.

The Pacific was not just the home of reprobates but also one of the great laboratories for biological ideas, attracting to its different regions T. H. Huxley, Charles Darwin and Alfred Wallace, the Holy Trinity of evolutionary theory. Wells was obsessed by evolutionary ideas and had been taught biology by the elderly Huxley, who died the year before *Doctor Moreau* was published. Much of Wells's science fiction plays with ideas of evolution and *The Time Machine* is both frightening and satirical about the idea, with its final glimpse of the furthest future when the earth will be inherited by gigantic crabs and then by 'some black object flopping about'. Only a few pages in, the original reader of *Doctor Moreau* would have settled back at this point (the Pacific setting, human seediness, the presence of animals), fairly confident that something grotesque and morally opaque was about to happen.

The genius of the novel lies in the way that, as in his other major books, Wells ruthlessly follows the logic of his story and does not really bother to fill in any needless details. Everything is infused with the same feeling of disgust. Already, simply as a man rescued from shipwreck, something is more than wrong with the narrator, who records that after his ordeal 'my eye caught my hand, so thin that it looked like a dirty skin purse full of loose bones'. In any other context this would just reflect a lack of food and water, but all his companions also seem to have terrible things wrong with them, which prove as nothing compared to what will be on the island. The brief description of his time in an open boat with his two (then) surviving companions also effortlessly raises one of the book's key themes: as they lie starving they realize that it is only through killing and eating one of their number that the other two can survive.

The battle to establish who will be eaten leaves Prendick both on his own and, through luck, at least temporarily released from some highly unattractive dining options. Once on Moreau's island it becomes clear that the dreadful things that lurk everywhere can only be kept in check through a system of religious prohibition that prevents their ever tasting blood. He meets Doctor Moreau, a vivisectionist who fled London after a scandal and has spent years on the island experimenting on animals to try to make them like humans. The island is littered with his experiments, some docile, some much less so, all of whom are under the control of The Law, a religion which is meant to direct their behaviour and keep them from reverting to the status of beasts.

I hesitate to wander too much further on to the island as it would be a pity to give away much more of its ghost-train atmosphere. Like a fairground, the island itself is pure pasteboard, bought cheap from Defoe's *Robinson Crusoe*, Ballantyne's *The Coral Island* and Stevenson's *The Beach of Falesá*. But its shoddiness is part of its joy – a barely sketched-in backdrop of bits of swamp, forest, a rocky cleft and volcanic vents, into which can be introduced an exquisite variety of spooky, half-glimpsed elements.

As to Moreau's base, it is unclear how the huge amounts of food, gear and laboratory equipment could possibly have reached it. It has some slight echo of Captain Nemo's submarine in *Twenty Thousand Leagues under the Sea*, which also roams the Pacific and seems to have similar supply and fuel headaches.

Moreau's antics and Prendick's gradual discovery of the emetic eco-system he has landed in form the core of the book. As Moreau's assistant tells him: 'This is a biological station – of a sort.' Like Wells's other early novels, *Doctor Moreau* is wonderfully replete with the love-hate relationships which characterized Victorian attitudes towards science. While we might ourselves be amazed at the Internet, it is in many ways simply a heightening, speeding up and improving of other technologies, whereas Wells was writing in an era where Christianity was under assault, Britain was invading huge chunks of the world, and in areas as various as electricity, surgery and astronomy amazing things were happening. Wells was as destabilized as anyone else by all this. Was there any limit to what science could do? Powered flight was just round the corner – but so were poison gas and artillery of a power and scale previously unimagined. *Doctor Moreau* is a game, but it is also a speculation about how we treat the natural world – or could treat it after yet another scientific breakthrough.

It is probably fair to say that all the films of *Doctor Moreau* have failed for the obvious reason that they are necessarily back-to-front. The doctor's experiments are to do with turning animals into approximations of human beings. These techniques not being in practical terms available to film directors, they are obliged to come from the other direction, by turning human beings into animals, through slightly more elaborate versions of putting on a pig mask held on by elastic. Wells's vision is of hyenas or leopards dreadfully fiddled with to make them talk and lurch about on spindly, spatchcocked back legs; no actor could be paid enough to reduce himself or herself to such irreversible ghastliness.

The 1996 film starring Marlon Brando as Moreau completes the appalling tradition. Brando, having brilliantly followed his own instincts to create the character of Kurtz in *Apocalypse Now*, felt that he could pull off the same thing in *The Island of Doctor Moreau*, reimagining the doctor as a figure inexplicably covered in white paint, white robes, dark glasses and a straw hat. He is accompanied by Nelson de la Rosa, one of the shortest men who has ever lived (two feet, four inches high). This grotesque movie was wonderfully made up for in 2014 by the derisive documentary about its making, *Lost Soul*.

Wells himself called *The Island of Doctor Moreau* 'an exercise in youthful blasphemy' and all the books in this great quartet of novels have a similar flavour. There is a glee in their inventiveness. *Doctor Moreau*, however, has a special intimate, literary quality – and who could resist a book where the seemingly sensible Victorian narrator is unnerved when 'something cold touched my hand. I started violently and saw close to me a dim pinkish thing'?

SIMON WINDER is the author of *The Man Who Saved Britain*, a book about James Bond's peculiar place in the British imagination, and a trilogy on the history of German-speakers and their neighbours: *Germania*, *Danubia* and *Lotharingia*.

A Hot-Water Bottle and a Horse

SARAH CROWDEN

Long before the term was used to describe talent-free people in the public eye, John Betjeman was a celebrity: Poet Laureate, saviour of ancient buildings and National Treasure. But though his wife Penelope is affectionately portrayed in his letters, and in a biography by their granddaughter Imogen Lycett-Green, for me she always remained an enigma. Until, that is, I was cast to play her in a BBC Radio production and discovered the first of her two books, *Two Middle-Aged Ladies in Andalusia* (1963).

Penelope Chetwode was a Daughter of Empire. Her father was Commander-in-Chief of the Indian Army, and, though born in Aldershot, she lived in India for extended periods as a young woman and again later in life. Her second book, *Kulu: The End of the Habitable World* (1972), chronicled her trek by mule in northern India. She also made a seminal television programme in the 1970s called *A Passion for India* and she wrote about the country for several magazines. How I should love to have met her. Refreshingly un-pc, yet compassionate, altruistic and non-judgemental, she was clearly completely without what used to be called 'side'.

Candida Lycett-Green's edition of John Betjeman's letters documents the myriad exploits of her doughty mother. Easily bored, Penelope was a restless soul who found many outlets for her vast energy. She was an inveterate volunteer and a pillar of the Women's Institute (making an impressive 70 lbs of jams and jellies in a single

Penelope Chetwode, *Two Middle-Aged Ladies in Andalusia* (1963)
Eland · Pb · 154pp · £12.99 · ISBN 9781906011680

season). She bred fowl, ran a popular café, entertained prodigiously and at one point wrote a cookery column. She also travelled extensively throughout her life and from childhood was a superb horsewoman. And though, like her husband, she was greatly loved, it's clear from *Two Middle-Aged Ladies* that she preferred horses to humans.

Courtesy of John Murray

Spain held little interest for her until the possibility arose of a solo ride in a remote region. Friends had long urged her to visit the country, and finally she was persuaded, both by them and by an article in a Sunday newspaper on conducted rides around Andalusia. The idea of a conducted ride in England would have been anathema to her, but Spain was another matter. After a preliminary guided excursion organized by friends, on 5 November 1961 she set off alone from Illora, north-west of Granada, to travel round and up the sierras of rural Andalusia, a trip of approximately 200 miles.

She stopped only at places she felt might be interesting. Sometimes she followed the Guadalqivir river which took her in an easterly direction, to her furthest point north, Torreperogil, and thence to the city of Ubeda, to view its magnificent architecture. From there she turned for home, meandering back to her starting-point. *Two Middle-Aged Ladies*, illustrated with her black-and-white photographs, is based on the diary she kept on the trek.

The ride was intended to be spartan – she took only a few clothes (a skirt for more formal occasions stored in a stocking to prevent creasing being my particular favourite), a hot-water bottle and a sturdy horse. It was an extraordinary undertaking, at a time when 'middle-aged' described anyone over 40, to ride alone over unforgiving terrain on an unknown mount in a country where she had only rudimentary knowledge of the language.

Airily dismissing the concerns of friends and family, she 'thanked

God for a plain middle age' which would stave off unwanted attentions. Her mount, the Marquesa, on loan from the Duke of Welling-
ton, a family friend, is described as 'equivalent in horse age' to her
rider, not beautiful but 'a good doer . . . the greatest blessing on a ride
of this kind', and blissfully unperturbed by strange stables and strange
company. It was she who turned out to be the object of endless attention from Andalusian men, natural horsemen all.

Penelope clearly approved of the basic accommodation provided
by posadas – inns with stables attached, 'the animals being often
better housed and better fed than the human beings'. 'Posada life
must be entered into in a spirit of adventure,' she observes. Most of
the bedrooms lacked glass in the windows and she often, without
complaint, slept in all her clothes to keep out the cold. Plumbing was
also virtually non-existent, and 'a po cupboard' a rarity.

She was a convivial guest, particularly when staying with families
where there was no posada. Here she was visited by curious villagers,
paraded at 'social engagements' and taken to other homes, once joining
in, willing as always to learn, in the preparation of pig's intestines (she
likens a ceiling festooned with sausages and black puddings to one by
Robert Adam, with added odour). The perfect day was one on which
she enjoyed 'an orgy of spiritual, gastronomic and aesthetic delights'.

Her intention was to keep to the Spanish equivalent of bridleways,
to satisfy her 'passionate desire for adventure . . . beauty and solitude',
using the sun to orient her. She was well aware that rural Spanish
roads with their many potholes would deter curious tourists, and she
would therefore be unaccompanied for much of the journey.

Only she could have taken with her as reading matter her daily
missal and Cervantes' *Don Quixote* – 'homework', read as she rode
(his 'lavatory humour' particularly appealed). Only she could have
set out with two almost illegible and conflicting maps, having researched her journey by consulting the works of nineteenth-
century fellow travellers in Spain, George Borrow and Richard Ford.
And only she, instead of counting sheep to get to sleep, could have

prayed to St Anthony (in French!) for the return of her Dayella pyjamas, lost from the saddle. St Anthony, of course, obliged.

A late convert to Rome, her faith sustained her, providing an immediate connection with priests and host families alike. Regular attendance at Mass, sometimes twice a day, helped her to master the language. Though self-critical about her linguistic abilities, she at one point discussed theology at length with a parish priest. Of the many churches in the towns and villages, she preferred the small, simple ones.

There is a charming, schoolgirl earnestness about Penelope Chetwode's writing; and the sheer stamina required to complete the journey, as illness and bad weather beset her, had me rooting for her. At one point she is tempted to turn back on an almost invisible and extremely hazardous path, but no, 'this was not the way the British Empire was won'. A quick prayer to the Blessed Virgin, and a man on a mule appears and guides her to safety.

Her respect for the country and its people grows. The relentless modernization of England and the disappearance of its traditions compare unfavourably with what she sees in Spain, and she robustly dismisses the canard that 'Spaniards are unkind to animals' when everywhere, clearly, the comfort of the horse is paramount. By 3 December, she is back where she began, having 'seen human beings as God meant them to be'. Her journey, a true act of faith, is over, its 'healing silence . . . like lanolin being rubbed into your soul'.

Penelope Chetwode died in 1986, on a riding tour in her beloved India. She was 76. How I wish she had written more. Thanks to her I have a renewed interest in Spain and, stamina levels permitting, I intend to go on pilgrimage to Santiago de Compostela. I shall wear stout boots, carry a dictionary and a copy of *Don Quixote*, and at my destination I shall raise a toast to those two adorable middle-aged ladies.

SARAH CROWDEN is an actress and writer who performs stand-up comedy as Dame Theresa Thompson's-Gazelle, also a Daughter of the Empire. And there the resemblance ends.

Labours of Love

PAUL EDWARDS

The words on Alan Ross's gravestone could hardly be simpler: 'Writer, poet and editor'. They could scarcely be more accurate either, although one wonders whether their subject might have given his commitment to poetry pride of place. Alan is buried in the church-yard in Clayton, the Sussex village where he lived for twenty-five years and where he knew great happiness. That happiness was particularly precious to a man who also experienced the fathomless miseries of depression. In *Coastwise Lights* (1988), his second volume of autobiography, Alan writes,

> Our house, which in its day had been successively Roman villa, farm and, more recently, rectory, looked westwards through an orchard, past Clayton church and farm, towards the great hump of Wolstonebury, whose slopes were rusted with beech woods. Sheer to the south the sky was bisected by the line of the Downs, crowding in and falling away as far as the eye could see.

Chelsea was another of Alan's haunts and his life in literary London also features prominently in the book; he lived in an Elm Park Gardens flat immediately after the war and died in a cottage in Elm Park Lane in 2001. This metropolitan base was essential for work: Alan was the editor of *London Magazine* for forty years, during which time he offered encouragement and hope to very many aspiring writers who wondered doubtfully whether a literary life was for them.

Alan Ross, *Coastwise Lights* (1988), is available as a Faber Find. We can also obtain second-hand copies of the original hardback edition.

Such blessings are still available to those who read his four volumes of autobiography or his other prose about travel, cricket and India. Poetry, though, lies at the heart of all his work.

Coastwise Lights begins roughly where *Blindfold Games*, Alan's first volume of autobiography, ends. Having recently left the navy, we find him in the post-war world attempting to make a living by writing. Yet even more than its predecessor, the second book tries to marry a broad linear narrative with a detailed account of episodes which encapsulated Alan's passions and style of life. This impressionism is even more pronounced in his next two volumes of autobiography, *After Pusan* and *Winter Sea*. The first begins with a thirty-page memoir of Alan's visit to the South Korean coastal city along with a consideration of the late nineteenth-century explorer Isabella Bird; it ends with eighty pages of poetry, the first Alan had written following prolonged depression. *Winter Sea* is subtitled 'War, Journeys, Writers' and is dominated by Alan's return to the Baltic, a sea in which he had nearly died fifty years previously. As always, there is poetry; as always, there is an insightful reading of somewhat neglected literary figures: the Norwegian writer Nordahl Grieg and the Estonian poet Jaan Kaplinski. These last two books are also briefer than either *Blindfold Games* or *Coastwise Lights*; perhaps they should properly be categorized as memoirs. But one is never surprised to find Alan stretching a genre, the better to reflect his experience, the better to accommodate the subtle rhythms of his prose.

These characteristics are abundantly displayed in the opening section of *Coastwise Lights*. We find Alan and the painter John Minton in Montparnasse, where they are staying in a cheap hotel en route to Corsica, the subject of their travel book *Time Was Away*. Already two of the autobiography's themes, travel and art, have been introduced. The title of the Corsican book is taken from Louis MacNeice's famous poem but *Coastwise Lights* is also interspersed with groups of poems used, as Alan writes in the preface, 'as illustrations and to fill in a few gaps'.

Readers expecting to learn much about Alan's adult family life might be disappointed by all four volumes of his autobiography. They will be told relatively little about girlfriends, wives, children. Family members are glimpsed in passing before their presence is

quickly woven into broader developments. This is not to say that personal relationships are omitted from *Coastwise Lights*. On the contrary, the book's richest theme is that of friendships, whether formed with painters like Keith Vaughan or authors such as Henry Green or William Plomer. Often one is sent back to writers one has heard of but does not really know. Like so many of Alan's books, *Coastwise Lights* can be an expensive purchase, not because it costs very much but because it leads one to curiously neglected authors from the second half of the last

Alan Ross by John Minton, *c.* 1947

century. For if a critic as tough and sensitive as Alan liked a writer, they must have something.

Alan's appreciation of writers like William Sansom or Bernard Gutteridge is warm but his assessment is unsweetened by fondness. Take, for example, this on Sansom:

On his bad days he could be taken for a bookmaker drowning his sorrows. There was an Edwardian courtliness to Bill's sober manner – and he was usually sober three weeks out of four – a bowing to ladies and a kissing of hands. He took to wearing a musky, extremely pervasive scent, which gave him a sweet, bear-like aroma. He tended to brush his rather fine hair straight back, not quite *en brosse*, but in the manner of an Italian tenor like Tino Rossi. I never saw it remotely ruffled, not even when he had fallen over.

Much of *Coastwise Lights* is devoted to descriptions of foreign travel. Alan was born in Calcutta, and his love of Sussex, where he was sent to school, was fostered partly by his need for an English *Heimat* and partly by his lifelong love of cricket. Yet he lost neither the urge to wander nor the desire to return to the South Downs. Kipling's lines, 'Swift shuttles of an Empire's loom that weave us main to main / The Coastwise Lights of England give you welcome back again' supply much more than a title for the book. They capture one of its essences.

Thus we begin with Alan in Montparnasse, looking out through the ventilation panel in the *toilette* of his cheap room and watching a domestic drama taking place in the apartment a few feet away. It is the sweltering summer of 1947 and all three participants he observes are naked. What Ross finds intriguing is the incongruity of the trio's behaviour; what the reader notices is the acuity of observation, the curiosity of the born writer. Other foreign trips are slightly more conventional but no less sharply realized. For four years Ross works for the British Council and accompanies its Controller of Education on a trip to Baghdad. On the flight from Rome to the Middle East he sits next to Agatha Christie. Eventually it is arranged that he will go on a shooting trip to the marsh country near Basra where he will enjoy the hospitality of the local sheikhs in their *mudhifs* on the banks of lagoons. He visits a now vanished world made famous by Wilfred Thesiger and Gavin Maxwell. 'The few days I spent in the marshes were a kind of dream, coloured the green of reeds, the blondness of corn, the gunmetal shimmer of water, the pale bronze of sky.' There are echoes of Edward Thomas here. The prose, as Ross recognizes, is often raw material for poems which are, to a degree, a different distillation of experience.

The trip to Iraq was Ross's first and last foreign adventure with the Council. Three years later he obeyed his obvious vocation and became a part-time freelance journalist. He had already published poetry, made translations and written essays on American authors, but the writing life was now the whole commitment and it remains a dominant theme of *Coastwise Lights*. While becoming well connected in the literary world – Harold Nicolson and Cyril Connolly were friends – he also expressed a then unconventional desire to write about sport. Before long he was filing football reports for the *Observer* and in 1953 he became the paper's cricket correspondent, a post he occupied for eighteen years.

Cricket writing, as some of those involved in it rarely recognize, is a niche activity. For every book which transcends the genre there are ten which remain clotted by statistics and routine match reports. What Alan succeeds in doing is taking moments on the cricket field and suggesting their relationship to other arts and different skills. One of his aims, as he wrote elsewhere, was to 'preserve a style, restore an action, rehearse an elegance'. The result is some of the finest cricket books we have and a body of other work in which style is bound to content. Cricket may sometimes seem a little distant but poetry is never far away. I am sure Alan would be happy with this. *Blindfold Games* is, he writes, 'an attempt to reconcile differing definitions of style and to trace the manner in which a single-minded devotion to sport developed into a passion for poetry'. *Coastwise Lights* continues that journey as the writer grows more confident in his gifts.

In 1961 Alan took over *The London Magazine* and changed more or less everything about it. The definite article was ditched, as was the dull cover. Under Alan's editorship coverage was extended to art, cinema, architecture and music. The magazine's archive, which is housed in the University of Leeds's Brotherton Library, contains hundreds of letters in which young writers ask Alan to consider their poems or short stories. The swiftness of the response was legendary and further correspondence is often filled with grateful appreciation of Alan's encouragement or acceptance.

The same library also contains the manuscripts of *Blindfold Games* and *Coastwise Lights*, many of the chapters written in the author's graceful hand on stationery liberated from distant hotels. One section of *Coastwise Lights* concerns Alan's involvement with *London Magazine* from the editor's perspective and chronicles the wide-ranging expansion into publishing which brought the work of Barbara Skelton, Julian Maclaren-Ross and Tony Harrison to a wider audience. 'Publishing has always been for me an amateur activity in the strictest sense of the word,' he writes; 'it was never my livelihood, nor have I ever earned a penny out of it. But, since it was a labour of love, there was all the more reason for it to be done to the highest professional standards.'

Coastwise Lights concludes with a section about horse-racing, another of Alan's passions and one facilitated in Clayton by the proximity of the small courses he loved. And so this book ends in Sussex with a description of village life and one of the finest final paragraphs in English prose. When serving on the deadly Baltic convoys in the Second World War, Alan had been sustained by the possibility of somehow returning to the county in which he eventually lived. The more remote that possibility seemed, the more vital it became to hold on to it. Earlier in *Coastwise Lights* Alan describes his move to Clayton:

During my sea-time I used to dream of Sussex; not so much a specific Sussex as a generalized romantic image conjured out of memory and hope. Sussex cricket played a large part in it, to the extent that I had only to see the word Sussex written down, in whatever context, for a shiver to run down my spine. Such an association might properly belong to adolescence, but it has survived. Now the dream was reality and for the next twenty-five years Sussex was my home, London a mere work-place.

Unlike the writers whose work he published, Alan is not in want of champions. For some cricket writers he is an example to which they might, on their best days, aspire. For writers of any sort, he manages, albeit after death, to offer something of the same encouragement he did when he ran *London Magazine*. Very recently, Gideon

Haigh wrote this about Alan's cricket writing: 'His work stands the test, I think, precisely because of the delight Ross took in his task, of crafting prose up to the standards of the players he was watching – a writer's writer, but of his subjects like an alert and observant partner.'

And then there is another writer. He has spent days in the Brotherton Library; he has wandered around Chelsea on murky autumnal evenings; and he has tramped the Downs around Clayton on summer afternoons when 'the landscape flows and brakes, chalk-slashed, tree-shadowed, its lanes dusty, partings in squares of corn'. He has done these things neither because Alan needs a biographer nor because he is, at least in part, a cricket writer. He has done them because he is fascinated with the mysterious process whereby one of his closest relationships has been formed with someone he never met; and because it is almost always *Alan* and hardly ever *Ross*.

PAUL EDWARDS is a former teacher who now spends much of each summer watching cricket and writing about it for *The Times*, *Cricinfo*, *The Cricketer* and other publications.

An Early-Flowering Climber

URSULA BUCHAN

When I was a student at Kew Gardens in the late 1970s, all my horticultural knowledge not acquired in lectures or through practical work in the gardens was drawn from the written word. A bookish childhood had given me a taste for fine writing, the more florid the better, which was not satisfied by the severely utilitarian prose of Percy Thrower, Roy Hay or Arthur Billitt, the bestselling garden writers of those days. I was driven to collect works by the prominent gardening writers of the previous hundred years, in particular William Robinson, Gertrude Jekyll, Frank Kingdon Ward, E. A. Bowles, Vita Sackville-West and, above all, Reginald Farrer.

Reginald Farrer (1880–1920) was unprepossessing in appearance, with a hare lip (the result of a cleft palate) only partially hidden by a moustache, a 'pygmy body' and a high, piercing voice. The son of narrowly Anglican parents (his father was a well-to-do landowner and Liberal MP, and the family were closely connected to the Sitwells), he was educated at home, at Ingleborough Hall in Clapham, in the Yorkshire Dales, and spent his boyhood gardening and searching for rare wild flowers on the nearby peak of Ingleborough.

Farrer went up to Balliol College, Oxford, in 1897, where things got much more complicated. He was desperate to be popular with his peers, but his waspish tongue put off those Olympian beings, such as

Reginald Farrer, *My Rock Garden* (1907), *Among the Hills* (1910), *The Dolomites: King Laurin's Garden* (1913), *On the Eaves of the World* (1917), *The English Rock Garden* (1919) and *The Rainbow Bridge* (1921) are all out of print but we can try to obtain second-hand copies.

Raymond Asquith, whom he wanted to attract. His deep feeling for Aubrey Herbert ('the man who was Greenmantle') was never reciprocated; indeed, it seems Herbert found his suffocating attentions a nuisance, not surprisingly. Then, in his twenties, Farrer converted to Buddhism, thereby alienating his parents, probably deliberately.

This temperament and his subsequent talent for mischief-making in print made many prominent gardeners wary of him. Nevertheless, he became a hard-working, practical plant nurseryman and a highly skilled botanist. He was also a gifted and assiduous plant-hunter, in the days when freelancers roamed the temperate regions, bringing back plants for British gardens. He was brave with it, for the Tibetan lamas, for example, whom he encountered on his travels in the Himalayas, deeply resented interlopers and could be fiercely hostile. The plants he collected on his travels included such staple garden stalwarts as *Viburnum farreri*, *Potentilla fruticosa*, *Daphne tangutica* and *Buddleia farreri* but also extremely rare Himalayan poppies and Alpine forget-me-nots and saxifrages. Despite his wish always to shine in company, he spent months on end alone, except for native servants, in remote places, seemingly content.

Although he aspired to be a novelist, it was as a gardening writer that he has had an enduring influence. He more or less invented the 'natural' rock garden, and certainly promoted it widely. And, posthumously, he inspired the foundation in 1929 of the Alpine Garden Society, which helped to foster generations of British gardeners devoted to cultivating difficult (or what Farrer called 'miffy') rock plants.

Among influential garden writers, I found no more intriguing, paradoxical individual than Farrer, nor one who excited in me compassion, admiration and exasperation in pretty equal measure. Although at times a conceited, thoughtless show-off, he was capable of inspiring deep affection in his (more pacific) friends, for he was cerebral, cultured and, intermittently, kind.

When I was a student I couldn't afford to be a bibliophile so, with the exception of his magisterial *The English Rock Garden* in two volumes, which cost me more than a week's wages, I possessed no fine editions of his work. I tended to buy one of the many cheap facsimiles that were published at a time before the Internet, when first editions of important horticultural works commanded high prices. (No longer.) The most thumbed of my facsimile copies is *My Rock Garden*, brought out by Theophrastus of Vermont in 1971, but originally published by Edward Arnold in 1907 – with many subsequent editions appearing until 1949.

What appealed to me about this, and indeed all Farrer's books, was his unselfconscious enthusiasm, which could sometimes elevate a pretty ordinary flower to heavenly status (especially if he had found it in the wild); his superb descriptive powers, borne of an observant eye and vast experience; his sometimes ridiculous flights of fancy; the precision of his instructions on how to grow alpine plants, which I believed implicitly; and his over-ripe, mock-heroic descriptions of his adventures in the European Alps and the Himalayas.

My interest in him became keener still after a visit to my elderly grandmother, who told me that she and my grandfather had stayed with Farrer at Ingleborough some time before the First World War. She said no more and it was only quite recently, while reading letters between the two men for my biography of John Buchan, that I realized the enduring bond between them. Buchan, the son of a Scottish Presbyterian minister, had always a tenderness for the lame and the halt, and he had known Farrer at Oxford, when the latter was probably at his most tortured. Farrer was unfit for military service, so Buchan, who became Director of Information in early 1917, sent him off to tour the battlefields of the Western Front and Italy and report back. Farrer collected his dispatches into a deeply poignant and heartfelt book, *The Void of War*, which he dedicated to his friend, 'the onlie begetter'.

In 1919, Farrer's magnum opus, *The English Rock Garden*, was published in two large volumes. It is an impressive achievement, written in prose that is witty and cultured as well as erudite. He then took

himself off to Burma with Euan Cox, a rhododen-
dron enthusiast, who had also worked under Buchan
during the war. Cox came home after a year, but
Farrer stayed on, botanizing in the rain-soaked fron-
tier ranges of Burma and China. Between January
and October 1920 he travelled a thousand miles, on
foot or on horseback, collecting 400 plant speci-
mens and writing field notes, dispatches for *The
Gardeners' Chronicle*, a full-length novel and a book
of 'historical fantasies'. He depended for company on the works of
his 'divine Jane' (Austen). In October he fell ill at Nyitadi with bron-
chial pneumonia. His servant ran four days without stopping to the
nearest source of medical supplies but arrived back only shortly
before Farrer died. He was 40 years old.

It is hard now to recapture the impact Reginald Farrer had on the
gardening world, since we don't make large rock gardens any more.
Modern anxieties about the conservation of water-worn limestone,
Farrer's favourite material, together with lack of professional gardening
help (for rock gardens are labour-intensive, as I discovered when I was
set to weed the one at Kew), have all but banished rockeries from
British gardens. Nevertheless, it is still fun to read *My Rock Garden*. In
it, Farrer electrified his readers by pungent and witty descriptions of
the three types of rock gardens that should *not* be made.

> The first is what I may call the Almond-pudding scheme, and
> obtains generally, especially in the north of England. You take
> a round bed; you pile it up with soil; you then choose out the
> spikiest pinnacles of limestone you can find, and you insert
> them thickly with their points in the air, until the general effect
> is that of a tipsy-cake stuck with almonds. In this vast petrified
> porcupine nothing will grow except Welsh Poppy, Ferns, and
> some of the uglier Sedums. The second style is that of the Dog's
> Grave . . . Plants will grow on this, but its scheme is so stodgy

and so abhorrent to Nature that it should be discarded. The third style is that of the Devil's Lapful, and prevailed very largely when Alpines first began to be used out of doors . . . The plan is simplicity itself. You take a hundred or a thousand cart-loads of bald square-faced boulders. You next drop them all about absolutely anyhow; and you then plant things amongst them. The chaotic hideousness of the result is something to be remembered with shudders ever after.

Sixty years after his death, alpine plant specialists were still talking about dogs' graves, almond puddings and devil's lapfuls. Moreover, in *My Rock Garden*, he first popularized the idea of the 'moraine' as a home for rock plants, an effective alternative to a rock garden, which can still be found in the gardens of enthusiasts, as well as in public collections such as the Botanic Gardens in Edinburgh.

His advice, though sometimes baroque and overblown in form, was severely practical and enlightened in substance. He brought back from his travels vivid memories of the conditions in which difficult alpines will grow. *My Rock Garden*, although it runs to less than 300 pages, cannot be read in one session since, after the introductory chapter, it consists mainly of descriptions of the looks and cultivation requirements of dozens of alpines and small perennials, a fair few of which have changed their names over the years. But it is the gateway drug to the rest of the Farrer oeuvre: of the others, I recommend particularly the plant-hunting books: *Among the Hills* (1910); *The Dolomites: King Laurin's Garden* (1913); *On the Eaves of the World* (1917); and *The Rainbow Bridge* (1921). You will encounter an opinionated, mischievous, but appealing individual, who never wrote a dull paragraph and always went his own way.

URSULA BUCHAN is a most timid plant explorer, but she still finds Farrer helpful and enlivening when she botanizes in the Alps.

Nothing but the Best

DANIEL WORSLEY

It was grudgingly that I started to read Iris Origo's *The Merchant of Prato*. My wife told me to. She had been referred to it for her studies. It sounded dry stuff, the re-creation of the life of a fourteenth-century Tuscan businessman from his account books and correspondence.

We had each been handed down copies of Iris's immensely readable *Images and Shadows* (1970) in which she describes how in the 1920s she and her Italian husband bought the derelict estate of La Foce south of Siena and painstakingly re-established the *mezzadria* system. This had been used in Tuscany from the days of the Roman Republic, the landlords providing the upkeep of the farms and paying for half of everything needed for cultivation, and receiving in return a half share of all that was produced. We had also retraced by bicycle Iris's fraught journey from La Foce in 1944, when she walked twenty-five refugee children she had taken in, along with the old people and babies from the farms, to the relative safety of Montepulciano, through the German front line under bombardment by the Allies as they fought their way north (*War in Val d'Orcia*, 1947; see *SF* no. 20).

The Merchant of Prato had initially been rejected by her usual publisher with the comment that it was hard to think of anyone who

Iris Origo, *The Merchant of Prato: Daily Life in Medieval Italy* (1957)
Penguin · Pb · 400pp · £10.99 · ISBN 9780241293928
Caroline Moorehead, *Iris Origo, Marchesa of Val d'Orcia* (2000)
Allison & Busby · Pb · 352pp · £9.99 · ISBN 9780749016562

might be interested other than medieval and Renaissance specialists; but in 1957 it was published in America, Italy and England, and received excellent reviews. Quentin Bell wrote to her describing it as a masterpiece: 'of late I have been . . . eking it out crumb by crumb in order to stave off the inevitable moment . . . when it was finished'.

Its subject, Francesco di Marco Datini, made a great deal of money. The son of a poor taverner, he was born in Prato, north-west of Florence, round about 1335. Both his parents died in 1348, the year of the Black Death. Aged 15, ambitious and curious but without backing or capital save the proceeds from the sale of a small piece of land, he set off for the papal city of Avignon, the centre of trade between Italy and Flanders, where there was already a substantial community of Italian merchants.

There he bought a shop, and soon expanded. Indeed, Avignon remained his centre of operations for over thirty years until he returned to Tuscany at the age of about 50. By the time of his death in 1410, twenty years later, he had many businesses and thriving *fondaci* – in Prato, Florence, Pisa, Genoa, Avignon, Barcelona, Valencia, Majorca and Ibiza. These *fondaci* were groups of buildings which were at once office, shop, dwelling and warehouse, with inner court-yards where the trains of pack animals would be watered and stabled.

Datini was a meticulous record-keeper, collecting every letter and business document he received and telling the managers of all his branches to do the same. In his will he left instructions for all these papers to be collected and preserved in his own house which, with his fortune, he left to the people of Prato. As Iris recounts in her introduction, the papers remained stuffed in sacks and left under the stairs. It was not until 1870 that some enlightened citizens of Prato brought to light this vast collection, which included business documents and accounts, and 140,000 letters. Of the letters, 11,000 were Datini's private correspondence with his wife and friends.

Iris came across the hoard when researching a paper about slavery in Italy in the fourteenth and fifteenth centuries and following the lead of a deed of sale to Datini of a Tatar slave girl. For two years she collaborated with a young Italian archivist, Gino Conti, who was able to decipher and translate the documents from their original early Italian and Tuscan dialect, and from them she put together a fascinating and detailed picture of the merchant's commercial, social and domestic life and attitudes, and intriguing portraits of his wife and friends. As Caroline Moorehead comments in her excellent biography *Iris Origo, Marchesa of Val d'Orcia*, one has to pinch oneself to remember that these documents portray life as it was over six hundred years ago.

From Datini's European network of *fondaci* and from further ports sailed the galleys that carried his wares: Cotswold wool, which by English law had initially to be shipped to Calais; salt from Ibiza; leather from Cordoba and Tunis; silk from Venice; lead and pilgrims' robes from Romania; sardines and honey from Marseilles; ivory and ostrich feathers from the Barbary coast; wine, bark and oranges from Catalonia; art from Florence; slaves from the Black Sea; dyes and spices from the Levant; vestments from Lucca; enamels from France; chessboards and maps from Barcelona; wheat from Sardinia and Sicily; coats of mail from Milan; swords from Toledo. It's an astonishing list.

Datini traded in the best. He had his agents secure the finest English wool from Northleach ('Norleccio'), Burford ('Boriforte') and Cirencester ('Sirisestri'). He was always on the lookout for a good deal, astutely anticipating the opportunities from breaking news, for example of an approaching famine, a treaty with the Turks or the election of a new pope. His *fattori*, or factors, on the spot managed the logistics, but he controlled them from a distance with his own untiring pen. As Iris writes, 'He was prepared to take great risks but diminished them by spreading them over the widest possible field.'

Personally, he was shrewd and mistrustful, not a serene or easy man. While making money he was perpetually anxious that he would

Francesco di Marco Datini
© Alamy

be cheated in his *fondaci* and by the people around him at home, and that his galleys would founder or be taken by pirates, though they regularly sailed in Venetian or Genoese convoys and with crossbow men aboard.

Then, when he had made his fortune, he worried that he would lose it; and finally, as he grew old, he was ridden by a gnawing anguish (or *maninconia*, as he and his wife call it in their letters) about the afterlife. At the head of each ledger is written 'In the name of God and profit'. The two were plainly not easy to reconcile. He lived in daily apprehension that none of his pilgrimages, fasts, gifts to convents or, finally, the bestowal in his will of his great fortune on his townspeople and the poor, would stand him in sufficient stead.

In contrast to Datini's brooding are the letters from his friend Ser Lapo Mazzei. In her introduction Iris describes him as 'the personification of the Tuscan virtues of piety and moderation – quietly counselling prudence and charity; proud of his friend's riches, but with no desire to share them, glad to enjoy with him a fat partridge or a glass of red Carmignano, but accepting no richer gifts – and gently striving, as the years passed, to loosen his friend's hold from the things he must soon leave behind him'.

> Often do I hear of your great banquets, for men and women rich in the vain things of this world; and that is good . . . But do not forget to let the poor, too, sometimes see your fine house, and be filled and nourished by your food, so that God may not reproach you, saying 'Had you but once asked *my* friends to the house I had given you!'
>
> I was glad that you took pleasure in my little kitchen-garden. I call it so, because so small a thing cannot be called a farm, but

to my mind, which desires but little, it is great enough. And this absence of desire seems to me the height of wealth.

Margherita, Datini's Florentine wife, was twenty-five years younger than Francesco and his social superior. After their return from Avignon he set her up at Prato, in a fine house he built, with a garden 'full of oranges, roses and other lovely flowers', though he later wrote that this had been 'a great piece of folly' for it cost no less than 600 florins – 'I would have been wiser to put it in a farm.' He was constantly then away in Florence or Pisa. They corresponded at least once a week about every detail of their domestic life and establishments, including their clothes and the washing which went back and forth by mule to Prato, and the fowls, eggs, vegetables and produce from the farm that she was required to dispatch to him each week.

The book concludes with chapters on the architecture and furnishings of the house in Prato (it is still there, preserved in accordance with his will), his farm, the couple's food, drink and health, and the plague and his ambivalent attitude to the Church.

Iris Origo's own life is also intriguing. She was restless, of an independent mind, courageous and scholarly. She wrote over a dozen books, including a life of St Bernard, but her publishers did not always find her easy to deal with. Caroline Moorehead tells this nice story, verified by the current John Murray:

> Jock Murray . . . had spent many hours grappling with Iris's squiggles. Coming back one day to his office in Albemarle Street he found the entire staff trying to decipher the last sentence of one of her letters. He took it home with him and put it on the edge of a table; the trick was, he said, 'to have the page at eye level, so I had a bath and a snifter, as Osbert [Lancaster] used to call it, and crept past the table on all fours'. The words now became perfectly clear: 'Dearest Jock', it said, 'I can't read what I have written. Please type it out and send a copy to me.'

Iris was the child of a wealthy and cultivated American father, who died when she was 7, and a mother of the Anglo-Irish Ascendancy. Her mother settled in Italy, and rented the Villa Medici in Fiesole where they became part of the literary circle which included Janet Ross, Edith Wharton, Harold Acton and Bernard Berenson, who lived not far away at I Tatti. She married Antonio Origo in 1924.

The destruction of all that she and her husband had achieved for the community at La Foce when the Communists came to power in Italy, after the Second World War, was an undeserved tragedy. Iris herself died in 1988 but the house and the garden she made at La Foce with Cecil Pinsent are still in the hands of her family, where they hold an annual music festival.

In a surprising way, it is Iris's way of life which has disappeared, and Francesco Datini's entrepreneurial opportunism which seems so contemporary – though the greed of the very wealthy no longer seems tempered by any fear of the afterlife.

DANIEL WORSLEY has never been a businessman, but he does have some Italian blood and he grows an olive and a few vines.

Keeping up Appearances

KATE TYTE

As a child I wore a lot of brightly coloured jumpers, frequently hand-knitted by my grandmother. They were itchy and they tended to shrink. Whenever I became trapped in one, arms waving helplessly above my head, my mother would tug it off crying, 'I can't *breve!* And the sleeves is all wrong!' The line comes from a scene in *The Family from One End Street*, in which a young boy named Jo becomes trapped in a shrunken jumper and multiple members of the family have to ease him out of it. The accompanying line drawing illustrates the problem perfectly. I don't know how old I was when my mother first read the book to me, but 'I can't *breve!*' soon became a family catchphrase.

Eve Garnett's children's novel was first published in 1937, with her own illustrations. At least eight publishers had rejected it on account of its supposed 'grittiness'. Here was a story about an urban working-class family that detailed the endless struggles of Mr and Mrs Ruggles – a dustman and a washerwoman – to feed, clothe and shoe their seven children. In fact the book was probably the first ever British children's book with working-class protagonists. Despite publishers' initial reluctance, it

Eve Garnett, *The Family from One End Street* (1937)
Puffin · Pb · 336pp · £6.99 · ISBN 9780141355504

was an immediate success. Serialized by the BBC in 1939, it won the Library Association's prestigious Carnegie Medal – beating *The Hobbit* – and has been in print ever since. In a market saturated with stories about boarding-schools, nannies and improbable Swallows and Amazons-type adventures, parents and children alike warmed to the novelty of the Ruggles.

Ironically, Eve Garnett's own childhood was more country house than One End Street. She was born at the manor house in a Worcestershire village and her father was a gentleman of independent means. She had a governess and later trained as an artist, including a stint at the Royal Academy. Despite her privileged upbringing Garnett became very aware of the social conditions of the poor. In 1927 she was commissioned to illustrate *The London Child*, a study of working-class childhood in the capital, and she also completed a forty-foot mural at the Children's House in Bow, in the East End of London. Though an upper-middle-class outsider, she was a careful and sympathetic observer of everyday working-class life.

One End Street consists of a series of simple vignettes. Its opening chapter describes the marriage of Mr and Mrs Ruggles, the birth of their seven children, and the difficulty of naming them all. The couple do battle over the eldest. Mrs Ruggles wants to name her Carnation Lily Rose after the painting by Sargent, which had caught her eye at the Tate Gallery on 'An-Excursion-to-London'. Mr Ruggles is still arguing against Carnation at the church door. Mrs Ruggles finally gives way and 'the screaming red-haired baby was christened, without further argument, simple Lily-Rose'. The poor girl is mercilessly teased at school because she in no way resembles either a lily or a rose.

Subsequent chapters are devoted to the adventures of each of the children in order of age. Twelve-year-old Lily-Rose tries to help her mother with the laundry – she is in the Girl Guides and wants to do a good deed – with disastrous consequences. Kate wins a scholarship to grammar school and loses her new school hat – the cost of which is carefully itemized – at the seaside. Nine-year-old twins Jim and John join 'The Gang of the Black Hand' hoping to have adventures. Seven-year-old Jo watches the first ever Mickey Mouse film in colour at the cinema. Five-year-old Peg doesn't have an adventure – perhaps it was hard to

imagine her getting up to much. But William, aged ten months, wins a prize in a baby competition. Finally the entire family go to London for a 'Regular Blow Out' at Whitsun Bank Holiday.

From these small, commonplace events the family wring all the entertainment they can. When Kate wins her scholarship the whole family celebrates with sardines and chocolate biscuits for tea. But grammar school involves expense, as Mrs Ruggles explains to Kate's teacher. 'I'm not one of these mothers what wants their children home and earning at fourteen . . . it's not *that* – it's the *clothing* of her!' The parents argue about which side of the family Kate's brains come from, and when Mr Ruggles completes a form for government assistance, he complains that it takes more out of him than two days' hard work. 'And you from such a brainy family – well I never!' his wife replies.

After a long series of mishaps Kate eventually gets her uniform. In the ups and downs of this episode the Ruggles could be any family: bickering, competing, anxious, teasing, forming alliances against one another, putting on a united front, sighing over each other's eccentricities and rolling out the same family catchphrases, handily capitalized for easy recognition.

Mr Ruggles and the older children are all 'afflicted with Ideas', much to Mrs Ruggles's dismay. Mr Ruggles keeps returning to 'The Question of the Pig' – whether there is enough space in the tiny back yard to keep one – while Kate dreams of becoming a pioneering modern farmer. Lily-Rose fantasizes about bossing workers about in her own modern steam laundry. Jim is a voracious reader of adventure stories from the public library. Then there's Londoner Uncle Charlie, a dustman who names his carthorse 'Bernard Shaw', attends a working men's college three days a week and thinks he might 'take it up political'.

The Ruggles family stand on the cusp of social change. My father was born in the 1930s and grew up in a world not so very different from the one portrayed here, a world that ended up offering, to his generation, unprecedented opportunities and upward social mobility. Rereading the book as an adult gives me a glimpse of his world and the sensibilities of his times, which are so very different from my own.

So many things about the working-class world of the 1930s amaze me. Clothes, food and all the small details of keeping up respectable appearances on a budget are lovingly described. When the Ruggles go to the seaside they choose a tea shop that allows them to bring their own bread and butter, so they can spend more on potted shrimps. Was it ever actually possible to go to a café bringing half your meal with you?

The children are astonishingly unsupervised and the parents are trusting to a degree that would be considered negligent today. Seven-year-old Jo spends all day outside by himself, with no one bothering to check on him. He indulges his passion for the Majestic Cinema on his own, with money he has secretly earned. Mrs Ruggles is cross if he misses dinner, but she never worries about him. And when nine-year-old John receives an unexpected invitation to a birthday party, his hosts send the following telegram: 'John perfectly safe; returning him tonight by seven o'clock bus.' How many parents today would feel reassured to receive such a message from a complete stranger?

Yet for all its emphasis on money worries, *The Family from One End Street* is still an idealized vision of small-town southern English life. At the time it was published it was already nostalgic. You wouldn't know from reading it that in 1937 Britain was in the midst of a depression, with mass protest marches against unemployment at home and upheaval abroad. This is an England centred on the church fête, not on factories and trades unions. When the children get into scrapes they are helped out by kindly adults, usually of a higher social class. After Lily-Rose shrinks a petticoat in the laundry, the customer laughs and plies her with cake. When Jo, Jim and John are discovered trespassing, the adults react with fondness and understanding.

Presumably that was part of the book's original appeal. An every-day world populated only by kind and forgiving people, with all ominous tension removed, must have been enormously soothing to contemporary readers in troubled times. It's still comforting today.

But not everyone saw it like that. Goebbels was so horrified by the poverty depicted in *One End Street* that he recommended the book as anti-British propaganda. After the war the Allied Commission suggested it as suitable reading material to fortify young German minds. By the 1960s intellectuals were scorning the novel as a patronizing comedy at the expense of the working class. Surprising, perhaps, for such an innocuous-seeming story about family life. But then again, what's a family without an argument?

KATE TYTE was an archivist and is now an English teacher in Lisbon.

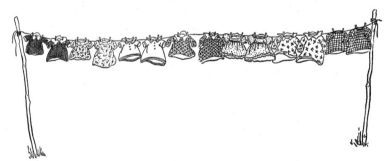

A Modern Prospero

BRANDON ROBSHAW

The Sea, The Sea was Iris Murdoch's nineteenth novel and the only one to win the Booker Prize (in 1978). It is, to my mind, her best novel, as well as being the most representative of her talents and distinctive world view. It is also hypnotically readable. Actually all her novels are hypnotically readable (with the sad exception of her last, fractured book, *Jackson's Dilemma*), but most contain certain faults of excess: passages of over-description, stagey scenes, unrealistic over-intellectualized dialogue, plotting whose artifice is all too obvious. This does not make them less lovable or less intellectually stimulating. Still: you can see the joins. This is not the case with *The Sea, The Sea*. In that novel Murdoch achieved the perfection of her craft. It is her *Great Expectations*, her *Mona Lisa*, her *Sergeant Pepper's Lonely Hearts Club Band*.

The opening sentence seductively draws you in: 'The sea which lies before me glows rather than sparkles in the bland May sunshine.'

That's beautiful. But in the very next paragraph things turn abruptly dark and mysterious: 'I had written the above, destined to be the opening paragraph of my memoirs, when something happened which was so extraordinary and so horrible that I cannot bring myself to describe it . . .'

What was it, what was it? Ah. We shall have to wait and see.

The bizarre, teasing, unpredictable plot (though *plot* seems too crude a word, somehow) is one of the great joys of this book. I shan't,

Iris Murdoch, *The Sea, The Sea* (1978)
Vintage · Pb · 608pp · £9.99 · ISBN 9781784875190

of course, disclose any details. Yet even when you know the story, *The Sea, The Sea* richly repays rereading (as do all Murdoch's novels, but this more than most). I have read it five times and I don't intend to stop there.

The story is told in the first person by Charles Arrowby (a number of Murdoch's novels feature a male narrator, none a female one). Arrowby is a famous and successful man, an actor, playwright and theatre director in his early sixties who has retired and moved to a lonely house near a desolate part of the coast, where he plans to lead a simple life and write his memoirs.

Of course, his life turns out to be far from simple and the memoirs never get written, at least not in the form he intended. Characters from earlier in his life reappear, crowding on to the pages. Typically for Murdoch, the dramatis personae are larger, more colourful, more vivid and more eccentric than real life. There's Lizzie Scherer, who is half Scottish and half Sephardic Jew, a former lover of Charles with 'the most adorable breasts of any woman I ever made love to'; Gilbert Opian, a gay, gossipy, somewhat ineffectual but very funny old actor who insinuates himself into Charles's household; the violent and unpredictable star of stage and screen Rosina Vanbrugh; her ex-husband Peregrine, a heavy-drinking Irish actor who specializes in TV villains; Charles's cousin James, an Army General and possible secret agent who is also a Buddhist; and Charles's first and only true love, Hartley, whom he has not seen for over forty years but who turns out to be living in the same village with her husband.

These are not just attractively painted caricatures. Murdoch does surfaces brilliantly, but what she is really interested in is the inner life. For her, morality is not only or even primarily about what you do, but about how you feel and think, your own internal view of others and how you attend and relate to them. She argues for this view as a philosopher in her book *The Sovereignty of Good.* Here, she makes the same point in literary form. Through Charles's observations we gradually come to see the motivations behind the machinations.

And nowhere do we see this more clearly than in the case of Charles himself.

Charles Arrowby is an example of a particular character that Iris Murdoch much enjoyed creating: the powerful man of superior gifts, will and intellect who dominates those around him. Other and later examples include Professor Rozanov in *The Philosopher's Pupil* and Marcus Vallar in *The Message to the Planet*. (It has been suggested that this type of character was based on Murdoch's own intellectual and sexual encounter with the philosopher and novelist Elias Canetti.) Usually Murdoch does not give the viewpoint to this person and we are never privy to his thoughts: we see only his effect on others.

In this instance, however, everything is filtered through Arrowby's thoughts and perceptions. Early on we are made well aware of his arrogance and egotism, his bullying and manipulative attitude to friends and lovers. As the novel progresses, cracks appear. We see his insecurities and fears, his remorse over past events and his blundering way of dealing with emergent ones. And we begin to like and understand him more, share and sympathize with his struggles as he makes his way through the 'demon-ridden pilgrimage of human life'.

The novel is full of Murdochian hallmarks. She is one of our great describers of nature and every few pages one encounters a description such as this: 'Enormous yellow-beaked gulls perch on the rocks and stare at me with brilliant glass eyes. A shadow-cormorant skims the glycerine sea. The rocks are thronged with butterflies.' Or: 'I was lying in tall luscious green grass which was just coming into pink feathery flower. The grass was very cool and dry and squeaked slightly as I moved.'

The Sea, The Sea also displays to the full her gift of describing while simultaneously reflecting upon physical sensations. It contains the best description of the experience of *falling* that I have ever read:

Falling, what the child fears, what the man dreads, is itself the image of death, of the defencelessness of the body, of its frailty and mortality, its absolute subjection to alien causes . . . My back and waist felt the dreadful imprint of the hands which with great sudden violence and indubitable intent propelled me over the edge. My hands reached out in vain for something to clasp. My feet, still touching the rock with which they were parting company, jerked in a weak useless spasm, a last ghostly attempt to retain balance. Then they were jerking in empty space and I was falling downward, as if my head and shoulders were made of lead.

Murdoch always excels at describing food, too, but in this novel she plays a strange trick on the reader. Charles Arrowby considers himself to be a connoisseur of the art of eating, yet the meals which he describes with such pride are weird, unappetizing little messes – chipolatas served with boiled onions and apples stewed in tea, kipper fillets sprinkled with dry herbs served with fried tinned potatoes, rashers of cold sugared bacon and poached egg on nettles. There is something both funny and touching about the enthusiasm and air of culinary expertise with which he describes these ghastly feasts; he confides to the reader that he used to think the only book he would ever write would be a cookery book.

Iris Murdoch loved Shakespeare with a passion, and allusions to his work run through all her novels. *Nuns and Soldiers*, for example, is full of parallels with *Hamlet. The Sea, The Sea* is plainly modelled on *The Tempest*. Charles Arrowby is Prospero, lone ruler of a sea-girt kingdom which is invaded by figures from his past (we are told that Charles once actually played Prospero in the theatre), and an alert reader can spot versions of Ariel and Caliban, as well as scenes of singing, drunkenness and a tragic drowning. But it's not just these literary echoes that show Murdoch's debt to Shakespeare. She is like him in outlook and sensibility. Her wide sympathies, her ability to understand and engage with every character, the way in which she mingles comedy and tragedy, and most of all her sheer interest in the daily process of living, the sensory experiences, the accumulation of detail by which she builds her worlds, the names of birds and flowers and animals and songs and pubs and wines and foodstuffs and books and works of art, her inexhaustible curiosity about the multifarious universe we inhabit: this is a profoundly Shakespearean way of looking at life and making art out of it.

The Sea, The Sea is a distillation of all that's best about Iris Murdoch's novels. It is excellent that she wrote twenty-five of them. But if you read only one, let it be *The Sea, The Sea*. If you are a newcomer to her work it is the ideal introduction, for it encapsulates all her virtues as a novelist, thinker and storyteller with none of the faults. If you know her novels already, then this is the most complete reminder of that magical, mystical, musical, marvellous Murdochian world.

BRANDON ROBSHAW lectures in literature and philosophy for the Open University. He has written a philosophical novel for young adults, *The Infinite Powers of Adam Gowers*.

Life among the Ledgers

PAULINE MELVILLE

I am rather fond of the crowd that Dante meets at the very start of his journey into Hell with Virgil. They are all rushing around moaning and shrieking on the edge of the River Acheron, hoping that Charon the ferryman will carry them across. He refuses. When Dante asks who they are Virgil tells him that they are the 'Futile', the people who have done nothing in particular with their lives. They are not well-known for anything. They have achieved nothing spectacular either good or bad. They are not allowed into Heaven in case their dullness dims the radiant light of Paradise, and Hell won't have them either because such an insipid bunch would downgrade the very notion of sinfulness. So they are not allowed passage across the river. They are seen hurrying to assemble under one flag and then fleeing in the opposite direction to assemble under another. They sound like most of us. Anyway, I number myself among them.

That early canto in Dante's *Inferno* set me thinking. I began to wonder what place the futile, the piddling and the paltry occupied in literature. Where were they? Did they ever come into their own? Could they rise to the heights of tragedy? Were they ever major protagonists in a story, being neither dastardly nor heroic, but just mooching along. The dastardly, in their dazzling darkness of evil, are well represented: Captain Ahab (more of Melville later), Shakespeare's Iago, Stavrogin in *The Devils*, child-killer Medea and indeed Satan himself in *Paradise Lost*. And it is only too easy to find swashbuckling

Herman Melville's 'Bartleby, the Scrivener' (1853) appears in *Billy Bud, Bartleby and Other Stories*: Penguin · Pb · 368pp · £9.99 · ISBN 9780143107606.

heroes and feisty heroines from Odysseus and Beowulf to Shaw's St Joan, Atticus Finch, Elizabeth Bennet, Anna Karenina, James Bond or Toni Morrison's Sethe. The list is endless.

But what about those who did not swash any buckles, those who just pottered along? Are they represented? Well, yes they are. Gradually, it dawned on me that the person I was seeking was that little-recognized creature who nonetheless inhabits some of the greatest works of literature. I give you the figure of the humble clerk. The first of them who springs to mind is Bartleby, one of the most famous of the species, described as 'pallidly neat, pitiably respectable, incurably forlorn' but who was destined for literary greatness.

Now that I look further I find that there are many of these figures scurrying about the pages of iconic works of fiction. I am not so interested here in those who have lesser, supporting roles, like the timid clerk Bob Cratchit in *A Christmas Carol* or the obsequious, insincere clerk Uriah Heep in *David Copperfield*. I am seeking those clerks who are the heroes of their own stories. Some of the most inspirational are to be found in Russian literature. There is Pushkin's clerk in 'The Bronze Horseman', who reaches the heights of tragedy as his life is swept away by the floods on the River Neva. Then we have Chekhov's 'Death of a Government Clerk'. Here the clerk's upsetting downfall and death are brought about by a mistimed sneeze at the opera. The government clerk in Dostoyevsky's *The Double* is driven mad by a lookalike who takes over his life. And how powerful these stories can be. Recently I picked up 'The Overcoat' by Gogol, having read it many years ago. It concerns yet another low-ranking government clerk whose coat is threadbare. By the time I was halfway through, and even though I knew how the story ends, I was so upset I could not bear to continue and had to put the book down until I felt strong enough to finish it the following day.

But surely the paragon, the nonpareil of clerkdom and life among the ledgers is Herman Melville's Bartleby the scrivener. (It is a complication for any writer to have the same surname as another more illustrious writer. I am often asked if I am related to Herman Melville. I am not. Although out of respect for my eminent namesake I have always refrained from writing a story about a big fish.)

Interestingly, whereas most of the clerks in Russian literature are state employees, Bartleby in the United States is employed in the private sector, in the Wall Street office of an elderly lawyer who has a 'snug business among rich men's bonds and mortgages and title deeds'. In fact, 'Bartleby, the Scrivener' is subtitled 'A Story of Wall Street'. It seems, without being overstated, that in his subtle and peculiar way, Bartleby had set his face against capitalism, which means, in America, against life itself.

The elderly lawyer is the narrator of the story. In answer to an advertisement for another scrivener to copy documents, 'a motionless young man' stands on the threshold of his office. It is Bartleby. He is placed behind a screen and does a prodigious amount of copying work in the first few days. But when he is asked to come out and examine a document with the lawyer he replies mildly from behind the screen: 'I would prefer not to.'

There is an exquisite delicacy in his refusal. He uses the conditional tense as if there were other possibilities. But there are no other possibilities. From then on he gives the same answer to every request, however small or reasonable, whether it is to assist in checking documents, copying a contract or running an errand. He always replies, 'I would prefer not to.' After a while he prefers not to copy any documents at all or accede to any other demand or entreaty. He is motionless in his passive resistance though unfailingly mild and polite. On being fired and asked to leave the office, he says: 'I would prefer not to.' It turns out he is living there. Often he is to be found standing motionless opposite a brick wall.

Faced with this genteel obduracy, it is Bartleby's employer who is finally obliged to move. Bartleby's behaviour is astonishing, infuriating, hilarious and profoundly shocking. The mildness of his manner contradicts the sheer effrontery of his inaction. Bartleby's pallid hopelessness becomes an emblem of tremendous power. His is the greatest of refusals.

Now civil disobedience is the active, professed refusal of a citizen to obey certain orders, wishes or commands of a government or some other authority. It has to be non-violent. It's possible to spot the first signs of such a tendency when a toddler in his high chair turns his face away from the spoonful of food offered by a desperate parent. Perhaps that is an early understanding of the power of refusal. Bartleby is, in his minor way, the forerunner of Gandhi. In fact, I sometimes wonder whether Gandhi did not have a copy of 'Bartleby, the Scrivener' tucked into his dhoti.

Herman Melville was born just over 200 years ago. Bartleby was one of the last pieces of published prose that he wrote. In an odd way the story seems to foreshadow the ensuing trajectory of Melville's own life. Bad reviews, poor sales, hostile critics – even for his earlier masterpiece *Moby-Dick* – meant that Melville gave up writing prose entirely and consigned himself to work as a customs officer for the remaining decades of his life. One of the greatest of all American writers preferred not to write any more fiction.

But the influence of Bartleby remains. Some years ago I was in Guyana on the northern border of Brazil visiting relatives. One evening we were at home under a palm-thatched roof from which the occasional lizard dropped to the floor. The community is Amerindian. People lay in their hammocks. Children sprawled on the floor. At the appointed time my cousin switched on the radio – only for a quarter of an hour in order to save the batteries – and we listened to 'Lillibullero' and the BBC World Service. That evening there was a poem by Andrew Motion about ice cream which left everyone stone cold. This was followed by William Blake's 'Tyger, tyger burning bright' which was listened to with huge pleasure, intensity and appreciation by those who were, indeed, more likely to come across a jaguar in their daily lives than an ice cream. For some reason, when the programme had finished, I decided to tell the story of Bartleby as far as I could remember it. It was the children who first spotted the possibilities. For a brief period the household descended into chaos as everybody 'preferred not to'. Later I heard that the idea had spread to a neighbouring village. None of it lasted, of course, but an idea has been planted that might one day have its uses.

For this reason alone I think Bartleby should be given permission to cross the River Acheron. His was surely an act of such glorious defiance that it deserves a place in either Heaven or Hell. Of course there would be others from the community of clerks who would be pushing and shoving to gain a place on the ferryman's boat. Mr Pooter the north London clerk would be among them, convinced that his *Diary of a Nobody* had turned him into a Somebody. Perhaps Chaucer's clerk, taciturn and thin as a rake (these literary clerks are rarely fat), would think of himself as a celebrity, given that he is still studied more than five centuries on. There would be a whole set of literary figures among the whirling throng of nondescripts trying to secure a place on that imaginary boat.

But Bartleby the scrivener's unswerving refusal to co-operate, his courage and persistence in disrupting daily life, make him a figure of incommensurable power who would surely be eligible for the journey. I see it now: Charon the Ferryman batting away the hordes of nonentities as they scramble to climb on board and then spotting Bartleby, relenting and offering him a place on the boat. And Bartleby's response? In Herman Melville's words:

'I prefer not to,' Bartleby respectfully and slowly said and mildly disappeared.

PAULINE MELVILLE has dual Guyanese and British nationality. Her awards include the Commonwealth Writers' Prize, the Guyana Prize for Literature and the Guardian Fiction Prize, among others.

Bibliography

Penelope Chetwode, *Two Middle-Aged Ladies in Andalusia*   57

Reginald Farrer, *My Rock Garden*; *Among the Hills*; *The Dolomites:
King Laurin's Garden*; *On the Eaves of the World*; *The English Rock
Garden*; *The Rainbow Bridge*   68

Theodora FitzGibbon, *A Taste of Paris, in Food and Pictures*   25

Eve Garnett, *The Family from One End Street*   79

John Harris, *No Voice from the Hall: Early Memories of a
Country House Snooper*   40

Charles Kingsley, *The Water-Babies*   7

Joan Lindsay, *Picnic at Hanging Rock*   19

Herman Melville, 'Bartleby, the Scrivener'   89

Iris Murdoch, *The Sea, The Sea*   84

Iris Origo, *The Merchant of Prato*   73

Christopher Robbins, *The Empress of Ireland*   13

Alan Ross, *Coastwise Lights*   61

A. L. Rowse, *A Cornish Childhood*   29

John Steinbeck, *Sweet Thursday*; *Cannery Row*   35

H. G. Wells, *The Island of Doctor Moreau*   52

T. H. White, *England Have My Bones*   46

Coming attractions

TIM PEARS uncovers family history in Poland · URSULA
BUCHAN helps out at her local library · ANDY MERRILLS gets
the low-down on Lyndon Johnson · HAZEL WOOD visits a
well-rooted small publisher · ADAM SISMAN goes back to
Middlemarch · CHARLOTTE MOORE hears the voice of Old
Russia · ROBIN BLAKE counts the cost of progress ·
SUE GAISFORD discovers the truth about Chaucer's Knight ·
DAVID FLEMING experiences a sinking feeling · LAURA FREEMAN
accepts an invitation to the waltz

Founded in 1761